Jesus Wept

Jesus Wept

REFLECTIONS ON VULNERABILITY
IN LEADERSHIP

Vanessa Herrick and Ivan Mann

DARTON·LONGMAN + TODD

First published in 1998 by
Darton, Longman and Todd Ltd
1 Spencer Court
140–142 Wandsworth High Street
London SW18 4JJ

© 1998 Vanessa Herrick and Ivan Mann

The right of Vanessa Herrick and Ivan Mann to be identified as the Authors of this work
has been asserted in accordance with the Copyright, Designs and Patents Act 1988.

ISBN 0–232–52276–6

A catalogue record for this book is available from the British Library.

The Scripture quotations contained herein are from *The New Revised Standard
Version of the Bible*, Anglicised edition, copyright © 1989, 1995 by the Division of
Christian Education of the National Council of the Churches of Christ in the United
States of America, and are used by permission, all rights reserved.

A concise version of the theology behind this book is contained in *Limits of Vulnerability:
Exploring a Kenotic Model for Pastoral Ministry* by Vanessa Herrick (Grove Books Ltd,
1997).

Designed by Sandie Boccacci
Set in 10¼/13pt Minion by Intype London Ltd
Printed and bound in Great Britain by
Page Bros, Norwich, Norfolk.

To Eilish

Contents

Foreword by Richard Harries, Bishop of Oxford   ix
Acknowledgements   xi
Introduction   xiii

PART I

1 The Way of Vulnerability   3
2 Living Vulnerability: Jesus Christ   9
3 Living Vulnerability: Prayer   20
4 Living Vulnerability: Community   35
5 Living Vulnerability: Leadership   49
6 Living Vulnerability: Humility   60
7 Living Vulnerability: Waiting   72
8 Living Vulnerability: Hope   82
9 Living Vulnerability: Trust   89

PART II

10 Prophetic Vulnerability: Professionalism   103
11 Prophetic Vulnerability: Ministerial Formation   117
12 Prophetic Vulnerability: Community, Leadership and
    Discernment   132
13 Prophetic Vulnerability: Leader and Community Together   143
14 Prophetic Vulnerability: Worship   160
15 Vulnerability: 'Place me with your Son'   175

Index of Names   185
Subject Index   188

Foreword

One of the reasons for the phenomenal response to Diana, Princess of Wales, and her death was her willingness to be vulnerable in public. If she had just been the embodiment of every girl's dream, a beautiful princess with life at her feet, she would not have had the impact she did. It was because on the one hand she seemed to have everything and yet on the other suffered in many ways and was willing to share something of this, that people responded in the way they did.

It is for the same reason that many of us find the tears of Jesus as moving as his joy. I love the Church of Dominus Flevit on the Mount of Olives, overlooking Jerusalem. Through the clear glass window behind the altar you can see the whole city spread out before you. It was here that Jesus wept when he was overwhelmed by the sense that the city did not know its time of peace. Here he seemed to foresee its future destruction.

Many of us were brought up on the philosophy of the 'stiff upper lip'. When I was sent away to school, because my parents were going abroad, I quickly brushed away my own tears in order to comfort my mother. But today, a greater emotional response is not only acceptable but widely regarded as more healthy, more human and indeed more Christian. So I warmly welcome this book and believe it will be a help to all who seek to follow Jesus in the conditions of today.

RICHARD HARRIES
Bishop of Oxford

Acknowledgements

We acknowledge the support and prayers of many people who have encouraged us as we have written this book. Our thanks go especially to David Moloney and Helen Porter, our editors at DLT, whose advice has been a constant help; to The Revd Dr Jeremy Begbie for his friendship, enthusiasm and wisdom as we tentatively explored the possibility of going into print; to John Beauchamp, Olive Barnard, Mike Tillett and the people of the parish where the book found its genesis; to staff and students at Ridley Hall, Cambridge; to The Very Revd James Atwell, colleagues and friends at St Edmundsbury Cathedral; to the Community of St Mary the Virgin, Wantage; to our families – David, Adam and Peter, and Catherine, Jonathan, Catherine, Michael, Patrick, Tizzy, Joseph (and Ebony the dog) – whose love, patience and practical support have made it possible for us to find time to write. Finally, to Eilish – thank you for being willing to accompany each of us on the Way of Vulnerability.

Introduction

'Vulnerable' is a fashionable word – but nobody says what it means. By reflecting on the example of Jesus Christ, the Christian spiritual tradition and pastoral experience, *Jesus Wept* seeks to recover an understanding of leadership (lay and ordained, 'sacred' and 'secular') which affirms a chosen vulnerability as a theologically valid and pastorally effective option for those who serve the wounded and risen Christ.

Part I explores the Way of Vulnerability. It suggests (in Chapters 2 and 3 respectively) that *relationship* and *prayer* are at the heart of following that Way, and that to follow it will affect the whole of life. Part II explores the prophetic role of vulnerability for all who lead, in both Christian and secular contexts, and for those who have responsibility for their selection and training. Although written primarily for those engaged in leadership in the Christian community, the truths it uncovers will challenge all who question the *invulnerability* of many in positions of leadership – whatever their context.

Part I

1

The Way
of Vulnerability

He stood. They watched. And as the flow of words ceased, the flow of tears began. It's not what you expect to happen in the middle of a sermon. It's not what you expect from a preacher at all. Energy, enthusiasm, a sense of conviction – even shouting. But not tears . . .

What should they do? What could they do but wait, until he was ready to go on? The silence seemed eternal for some. One coughed, another, betraying her discomfort, rustled a service paper, and dropped it. Others watched as he allowed the tears to fall.

They watched, and after a while he continued. And they listened the more intently, because they knew that these were no mere words, hurriedly put together the night before. These were words expressed by a man who was prepared to make a fool of himself, who was prepared to risk appearing weak and 'out of control' in front of three hundred and fifty people in the congregation that day. Some were alienated completely. Others saw the tears of Christ.

But should it have happened at all?

To see a man in tears is relatively unusual. Even in a Western culture where many of the stereotypes of gender can no longer be taken for granted, it is still an uncommon occurrence. To see a man – or, indeed, a woman – who is responsible for the conduct of Christian worship and preaching in tears would be considered by some to be totally inappropriate: a failure to exercise necessary responsibility and control, and an undermining of their leadership and the authority invested in them. At best, such a display might depict a leader under severe strain, one who should be encouraged to 'step down' until the pressures have eased. At worst, it might depict a leader who seeks to manipulate a congregation by deliberately using an over-emotional approach.

Or perhaps there is another possibility . . .

Perhaps such a 'display' is not a display, in an active sense, at all. Perhaps it is, rather, a willingness for things to be seen (for a moment at least) exactly *as they are*. Perhaps it is a decision, a choosing, to put aside the mask; to strip off, for a time, the protective clothing of status and the expectations of others. Perhaps it is a resolve to risk transparency, and choose to follow the way of vulnerability. For somewhere between the tears of strain and the tears of manipulation are the genuine tears (whether they are allowed to fall or not) of the humanness of those who are called to lead the Christian community. It is the question of whether and when and under what circumstances those tears are allowed to flow that forms the substance of this book. And not simply 'tears' in the narrow sense, but the broader possibility of the apparent weakness and vulnerability which they may convey. In short, what is the place of vulnerability in Christian ministry, and for Christian leaders especially?

'Vulnerable' is a fashionable word. One of the problems with fashionable words is that they are used widely, and loosely, in many different contexts and with a variety of meanings. Sometimes the word 'vulnerable' is used in a negative sense to describe – often in a somewhat patronising way – individuals or groups who are deemed to need extra 'protection': for example, children, the elderly, those who are physically or mentally handicapped, or those who are materially poor. Sometimes it is used in a positive, almost indulgent way to describe an openness of relating which seems actively to seek painful encounter with another.

The *Shorter Oxford English Dictionary* (Vol. II, p. 2375) traces the roots of the word 'vulnerable' to the Latin 'vulnerabalis' and the verb 'vulnerare', 'to wound'. Rarely is this verb used in the active sense of 'having power to wound'. More commonly it is used in a passive sense to describe 'that which may be wounded or susceptible of receiving wounds or physical injury'. But its meaning is broader still, for it is used in a figurative sense to describe someone who is 'open to attack or injury of a non-physical nature'.

4

A word's popularity may not only cause people to wonder what it means but also lead to its losing its impact. When those in caring professions speak about vulnerable people, and politicians refer to the vulnerable groups in society; when newscasters speak matter-of-factly of refugees and victims of terrorism, and financiers and industrialists speak of a vulnerable economy, it is easy to lose any real sense of being wounded and the pain it may bring to those concerned.

'Vulnerable' has even become a fashionable word in recent Christian writing. Many people use the word and yet none of them define what they mean. Understanding is assumed. Their approach would seem to suggest that since humanity's healing is 'by the wounds of Christ' so the ministry of healing (in its broadest 'salvific' sense), to others, will also be through the weakness and vulnerability of those who are leaders and pastors of the Christian community. But what is this vulnerability? Is it a way which all Christian leaders are called to follow or only a few? How does 'vulnerability' fit with authority and the exercise of power? Was Jesus really vulnerable and, if so, in what way and to whom? Should this be a pattern for Christian leaders? Indeed, can it be?

For the sake of clarity we shall define vulnerability as

An openness to being wounded (physical or otherwise) which is motivated by love of God and is the outcome of a voluntary relinquishment of the power to protect oneself from being wounded.

Its two components are thus potential pain (in whatever form – physical, emotional, spiritual – that pain may take); and 'choosing' – the choosing to open oneself to the possibility of being wounded, of being hurt, of being thought incompetent and a fool. And all this for love. Pain and choice. Vulnerability, in the sense in which we are using it, involves a measure of control. It is a way we can choose to follow or not – which is not to suggest that pain will be avoided if we go for the 'safer' way. Neither the potential for suffering nor the depth of God's love for us is dependent upon our choosing one way or another. Yet to choose the way of vulnerability is to assent to God's choice. It is to allow the self to be seen and not hidden behind

a shell of professionalism, control, skill and technique. It is to lay ourselves open to the one who laid himself open to humanity. It is to learn how to relate appropriately to others. It is to rediscover the place of humility; to recognise the value, sometimes, of choosing not to act. It is to begin to understand that to be vulnerable is to be a sign of hope.

And to walk the way of vulnerability has implications for the whole of discipleship – for prayer, for life in community, for leadership. It may question the way in which vocations are discerned and by whom. It challenges the professional, technique-orientated approach to training leaders in the Christian Church which has dominated the last twenty years.

Yet, the way of vulnerability is not another technique to learn as part of 'ministerial formation'. It is the living of a life which has a desire for transparency to the things of God. It is an openness to his ways of handling any situation; not relying on our own unaided judgements but allowing our reason and our logic, our experience and our training to be informed afresh, to be turned over, if necessary, by the discernment of and obedience to the voice of love, that voice of God which alone directs our way. 'This is the way, walk in it' (Isa. 30:21).

It is a way, too, which is guided by a vision of God and his Kingdom and which seeks 'heart-knowledge' of God, that deep knowledge which is allowed to inform the head but is itself the product of allowing the head to enter the heart and be loved into new life. It is a vision which embraces the whole of our being in the pursuit of the vision of God and in the mission of calling others to that vision, that vision of God revealed in the face of Jesus Christ.

It is this vision which brings a unity to our living and our praying, our ministry and our life. It is the vision which undergirds the ministry of Christ. He constantly looked to the Father and he constantly attracted others to share the loving gaze which he enjoyed. To be vulnerable to God in this way is to be vulnerable to love, to being loved even beyond our sin, beyond our frailty, and to share that depth of love, that knowledge of love with others. It is to weep with those who weep and rejoice with those who rejoice, and not to be ashamed.

In other words it is to be fully alive. St Irenaeus caught it all perfectly: 'The glory of God is a living man; and the life of man is the vision of God.'[1] Vulnerability is not about a negative attitude to oneself or life but rather about living our truth before God and for the sake of others. It is about letting go of all falseness and avoiding any kind of stagecrafted religiosity. There is no room for a pious shrinking from life but a call to live beyond what we see and hear and touch and feel, to live God's life in this life, to live the Kingdom in the present. It is to live through hell and still live in heaven, to believe that beyond all the world's false glamour, sham and broken promises there is a purposeful and loving God who cares intimately and uniquely for every single scrap of humanity and for all of his creation.

St Augustine says 'We are Easter people and Alleluia is our song', but Easter people live in a world, in a church, and in relationships and bodies which know the frailty and the pain of humanity. To live as Easter people requires vision and grace. It demands of us that we do not try to avoid the world's pain and darkness but rather bear it and even dare to bear it for others, believing that all darkness, all suffering, all agony and dereliction can be redeemed. To live this way is to trust absolutely in the Father's love, as Jesus trusted. It is to believe that, in God, nothing is wasted. It is to believe, to know intuitively and surely, that life without God is not life but a weak reflection of what life can be. Without such a vision, people perish. Without some meaning to life, suffering is intolerable. Without vision, vulnerability is a fool's errand.

It is time for the heart to enter again the head, to take the vision into the arena of reason and intellect and to explore how this concept of vulnerability finds its *raison d'être* not just in our felt experience but also in our theology; for although the word 'vulnerable' has become so fashionable, little attempt has been made to root it biblically and theologically. We hope that the pages that follow may begin to do so. It is our conviction that in Jesus Christ we see the way of vulnerability lived out most fully, in his choosing to come in human flesh, to live and die and rise again. His 'Yes' to his father – again, and again, and again – led both to his self-emptying (Phil. 2:7) and to his suffering and death. In his choosing to be vulnerable to those around him, he opened the way for others not only to do their worst to him but also to see him as he really was. Not a cardboard cut-out of a Jewish rabbi, but in his full humanity as one who lived and loved and laughed and cried. It is, as always, he who must be our starting point.

We gaze at Christ, crucified and risen, himself vulnerable to the wounds of nail and lance and anger spat at him by jeering crowds. St Ambrose writes, 'It is important to consider in what condition he ascends the cross, for I see him naked.'[2] The vision is of a Christ who hangs naked before us, unafraid to be naked and vulnerable because he stands naked before the Father's love.

To follow such a Christ is to allow God to strip you, to let him make you vulnerable to his love in your ministry.

> *He stood. They watched. And as the flow of words ceased, the flow of tears began . . . Jesus began to weep. So the Jews said, 'See how he loved him!' But some of them said, 'Could not he who opened the eyes of the blind man have kept this man from dying?'* (John 11:35–7)

NOTES
1. Kenneth E. Kirk, Adv. haer., iv, 20.7, quoted in *The Vision of God* (London, Longmans Green & Co., 1931), p. 1.
2. Quoted in Martin Thornton, *A Joyful Heart* (London, SPCK, 1986), p. 30.

2

Living Vulnerability:
Jesus Christ

I see a wonderful kind of love!
Thy Highness lieth in the straw:
the hands that made the world
make tiny gestures in a Mother's arms:
the eternal Wisdom, of his own will,
is powerless to speak, to think.
Whoso is wise will ponder these things
and understand the loving kindness of the Lord.[1]

A Condescending God

There are few more powerful images of vulnerability than a new-born baby; and the child's defencelessness and utter dependence on those who care for him are heightened when the circumstances into which he is born are, in themselves, vulnerable. Such an image can still have an impact even on *our* dulled consciousness when we recognise that it may be happening only a few miles away in our local community. Yet sometimes we become numb, and fail to acknowledge the reality of many of the births which have taken place and which still take place in our world without warmth, security and medical support but, rather, exposed and lonely and vulnerable.

The comfortable images on Christmas cards, in Victorian carols, in the infant-school nativity play – even in the neatly crafted Christmas crib – depict a birth far different from that which took place in the stable of Bethlehem. This was not a comfortable birth: to be born amongst a people under oppressive rule, in particularly

9

difficult circumstances, temporarily homeless, and to a young first-time mother, as yet unmarried to the man who was not even the father of her child, wasn't exactly the ideal point of entry into the world. And yet this was the way God chose.

The story of Jesus' birth, as it is recorded in the gospels, is a strange mixture of the amazing and the ordinary. St Luke, in particular, combines the wonder and enormity of this event of cosmic significance with the down-to-earth reality of the circumstances into which Jesus Christ was born. For the social and physical contexts of Jesus' birth express a vulnerability, poverty and insignificance strangely at odds with the angels' words of acclamation to the shepherds:

> to you is born this day in the city of David a Saviour, who is the Messiah, the Lord. This will be a sign for you: you will find a child wrapped in bands of cloth and lying in a manger. (Luke 2:11–12)

'A Saviour . . . the Messiah, the Lord', whose arrival is announced by a multitude of the heavenly host; a king whose coming has been foretold, expected and anticipated by thousands, and yet who, when born, is wrapped in bands of cloth, laid in an animal's trough, in a back-street cave in an insignificant town on the edge of the Roman Empire. Here is no special protection or immunity. Here God is enfleshed in the weakness of a vulnerable child. The world may have been waiting for a king (Matt. 2:2). The king who came was poor and weak, and went unrecognised except by those to whom the Spirit made him known: Mary (Luke 1:31), Joseph (Matt. 1:20f), the shepherds (Luke 2:15,20), the wise men (Matt. 2:11), Simeon and Anna (Luke 2:26f). They saw through the weakness and vulnerability of the child to the revelation and glory and majesty of the condescending God.[2]

The paradox of this 'divine condescension' lies at the heart of the incarnation. How could God become a vulnerable human being and still be God? And if he *was* still God, then was he really human? How *could* the humanness of Jesus Christ be the same as yours and mine?

To be more specific: if Jesus Christ came in the flesh (as the gospels tell us he did), as a vulnerable, human child, was he *really* vulnerable

– the same as any new-born baby – or only pretending to be? Was his vulnerability the same as ours? Or did he have some extra layer of protection – some sort of 'divine bubblewrap' – because he was God, and God could not afford anything disastrous to happen to *this* particular baby? If he was specially protected, then surely his humanity was not the same as ours. We are not encased in 'divine bubblewrap'! What use is he as a model for *our* vulnerability, and how can we identify with him, if he was somehow different from us? Equally, if Jesus really was just the same as you and me, then how can we say he was 'God made flesh'? He may well have experienced, identified with and shared in the frailty and weakness of vulnerable humanity, but how could he then, at the same time, have been the perfect instrument of that same humanity's salvation?

These are enormous questions which have exercised the minds of enquiring people through the centuries. But why do they matter? They matter because if (as we suggested at the end of Chapter 1) it is Christ who must be our 'starting point' for exploring the way of vulnerability, then we have to be sure that he is someone with whom we can identify, someone whose vulnerability is *real*, and (more importantly, perhaps) someone who can identify with us in *our* vulnerability. It is no good gazing at Christ through bubblewrap: we have to be sure that he felt the nail and the lance, the ridicule and the abuse. Only then can we begin to entrust ourselves to him in our vulnerability.

As we begin to look at this 'condescending God' more closely, we recognise that of ourselves we cannot make ourselves like him. To assume that we could would be arrogant blindness! We cannot 'imitate him' in the sense of copying him or matching up to him.[3] We can only, by his grace, 'be imitators of him' (1 Cor. 11:1; 1 Thess. 1:6; John 10) in a dynamic way, as, enabled by the Spirit, we offer ourselves continually as channels of the Father's love to the world. It is *he* who makes us like himself – and not we ourselves! Jesus Christ was born as a vulnerable baby at Bethlehem, and lived a fully human life 'yet without sin' (Heb. 4:15). Whatever the strength of our love, and however Spirit-inspired we may be, our motives are always mixed and impure, and we are always susceptible to sin. Only the Son of God was motivated by pure love and service of his Father and of humanity. And for Jesus Christ, to be vulnerable was an expression of a love which would lead to death. No passage in Scripture captures this more beautifully or more succinctly than Philippians 2:1–11. It is to the picture of Christ in this 'classic' passage which we must turn our gaze – to the picture of the self-emptying Christ – for it is there that we may discover more about what it meant for the eternal Son of God to become a vulnerable human being.

The Self-emptying Christ: Philippians 2:5–8[4]

5. Let the same mind be in you that was in Christ Jesus,
6. who, though he was in the form of God,
   did not regard equality with God
   as something to be exploited,
7. but *emptied himself,*
   taking the form of a slave,
   being born in human likeness.
   And being found in human form,
8. he humbled himself
   and became obedient to the point of death –
   even death on a cross.

The key phrase, for our purposes, occurs in verse 7 – 'but *emptied himself*'. As always, however, it is important to look at the phrase in the context of the whole. Why did Paul write (or quote) this passage to the Philippians? What might his purpose have been? The answer to that question lies in the four verses which precede this passage, and in verse 5 especially: 'Let the same mind be in you as was in Christ Jesus.' St Paul was encouraging his readers to model their corporate, daily life on the example of Jesus Christ. His 'mind' or 'attitude' is to be theirs. And so the verses that follow are set in this practical context. St Paul was not writing a set of doctrines (although, clearly, what he says has great doctrinal significance!). No, he was writing practical theology: 'Be like Jesus Christ in your attitudes to one another in the community, and live out those attitudes appropriately, even if that means *loss of status, becoming low, becoming a slave,* and even if that means losing your life for the sake of the other.' In short, allow yourself to be vulnerable, like the self-emptying Christ 'who became obedient to the point of death – even death on a cross' (v. 8).

So the context for the passage is a practical one. Nevertheless, it matters (and not just from the point of view of Christian doctrine) what it means. What is this self-emptying, and what does it mean when we speak of it alongside our earlier questions about how God could be both fully God and fully human? Was the incarnate Son's divinity somehow modified in order for him to become the human Jesus, or was he merely pretending to be human? Was he vulnerable or not? Did he put his divine powers 'on hold', as it were, for the time he was on earth, or did he abandon them altogether? And if he 'emptied himself', what was it that he emptied himself of? Did some change of 'being' or 'substance' take place when God was conceived in Mary's womb, only to be reversed at the resurrection? Or should we be thinking less about change of 'being' or 'substance', and more about 'attitude' and 'relationship'?[5]

These questions became particularly pertinent during the nineteenth and early twentieth centuries, when theologians (especially in Germany and England) were trying to reconcile their new-found interest in the historical Jesus, and their new-found psychological insights, with a desire (on the part of some of them at least) to retain the divinity of the incarnate Son. So emerged what has come to be known as Kenoticism, a word which derives from κενωσις, 'kenosis', the Greek for 'self-emptying'. Here is not the place to focus on the intricacies of Kenotic Christology; suffice to say that a wide range of suggestions were made over a period of about seventy years (c. 1850 – c. 1920) concerning the complete or partial renunciation or 'veiling' of some or all of the incarnate Son's attributes of divinity.

The Kenoticists were, however, looking at the problem in the wrong way. Their understanding was blinkered by thinking of Jesus Christ as human and/or divine in purely *substantial* terms – a case of being either human or divine. For them, Christ's self-emptying had to be about some substantial change; most usually, about some loss of the divine in order for the human to be acceptable. Karl Barth (1886–1968), however, offered an alternative approach to Christ's self-emptying: 'The kenosis consists in a renunciation of his being in the form of God *alone* [my italics].'⁶

For Barth, the self-emptying was, paradoxically, a 'taking on' – a choosing to take 'the form of a slave' (v. 7), something which Barth understood not as a loss of divinity, but rather as a particular expression of that divinity which enabled God to interact with humanity in the person of Jesus Christ in a way that was both faithful and appropriate. Jesus Christ was no less God (Barth could not have entertained such a suggestion!),⁷ and yet in his time as a human being on earth his attitude towards his divinity was such that he never took advantage of it, but lived a fully *human* life. The divine encompassed the human, but did not stifle it or swallow it up.⁸ Thus the self-emptying of Jesus Christ was about self-negation, about making himself powerless, about becoming vulnerable; not because he had to (he was, and never ceased to be, *God* throughout his time on earth), but because he chose to. In so doing, he did not negate his divinity, but rather fulfilled it, because that was how he most appropriately and faithfully expressed his divine equality *in the human context.*

Barth describes this choosing to take on the frailty of humanity in terms of the eternal Son going into the 'far country'.⁹ Alluding to the Parable of the Prodigal Son, he sees the incarnation as the Son's journey into the place of fallenness and pain; the entry into the 'strange land' from which he later returns after suffering and humiliation, to restore fallen humanity to the bosom of the Father, and to share in the Father's glory (cf. *Church Dogmatics* IV. 2.64.2 pp.). Yet whilst in this 'strange land' he remains fully the eternal Son:

He humbled himself, but he did not do it by ceasing to be who He is. He went into a strange land, but even there, and especially there, He never became a stranger to himself. (*Church Dogmatics* IV. 1.59.1 pp. 179–80)

From our brief study of Philippians 2: 5–8 and of Barth's approach to the topic, then, two clear principles emerge. Firstly, the incarnate Son's 'self-emptying' was a matter of choice: he was not 'emptied'; rather he 'emptied himself'. Secondly, his self-emptying was an act of obedient love to the Father, the consequence of which was suffering, humiliation and death. Choice and pain. Pain and choice – seen in Jesus Christ, and in all who follow the way of vulnerability.

Yet what is it that made it possible for Christ (and makes it possible for us) to choose to follow that way?

A 'Relational' Approach: the role of the Holy Spirit

We have seen already how Karl Barth saw beyond the intractable difficulties of understanding the divinity and humanity of Christ in terms of 'substance' and 'being' by speaking of Jesus as, in some way, 'taking on' humanity because that was the only way in which he could faithfully relate to humanity. For Barth, the *expression* of God *to* humanity (that is, how God revealed himself to and related to humanity) was as important as the *being* of God *as* humanity.

Nearly two hundred years earlier, the Puritan Divine John Owen had recognised the importance of understanding how Jesus could be both divine and human in 'relational' terms. In his article 'Christ's Humanity and Ours: John Owen' (1991), Alan Spence[10] presents Owen's understanding that Jesus was to be regarded as 'the prototype of Christian existence, and as continually empowered, comforted and sanctified by the Holy Spirit' (p. 75). For Owen, 'the eternal Son *assumed* human nature into personal union with himself, but . . . all direct divine activity on that assumed nature was that of the Holy Spirit' (ibid., pp. 75–6). Thus, for example, it might be argued that Jesus' baptism by John was unnecessary: if he was divine, and already in relationship with the Father and the Spirit, then why was it necessary for the Spirit to 'descend on him in bodily form like a dove' (Luke 3:22)? The answer is that in his humanity the incarnate Son was as dependent on the Holy Spirit as any other human being. It was thus possible to conceive of the incarnate Son, Jesus Christ, as both fully human and fully divine, not because of any metaphysical change which may have taken place but because the Holy Spirit enabled him to relate to the Father *in his humanity*. The *eternal* Son was thus in relationship with the Father and the Spirit by virtue of his divinity, and the *incarnate* Son was in relationship with the Father, *by means of the Spirit*, in his humanity.

This has important implications for us because we too have access to the Father by means of the Holy Spirit. If the incarnate Son could choose to be vulnerable, then so might we. In the Spirit, we have precisely the same resources of grace and discernment as did the incarnate Son, Jesus Christ. We are not divine, as he was, and yet his humanity and ours are alike; his joys and ours are alike; his weakness and ours are alike (cf. Heb. 4:15–16). Not only that, but (just as he did for the incarnate Son) the Spirit enables us to relate to our fellow human beings in ways that are appropriate. We can tend to want to live life by set patterns and set rules. If we begin to see the value of choosing to make ourselves vulnerable to others, it can be tempting to believe that that is always going to be the appropriate way to behave. Jesus did not treat everyone uniformly. He respected the uniqueness of each individual, and so should we – something we shall explore further in due course.

The work of the Spirit in relating is thus vital; both in terms of relationship with the Father, and in terms of relationships between human beings. It was so for Jesus Christ, and it is so for us. For Jesus, the Spirit's work was not solely in terms of power and resource (although it clearly *was* that – Luke 4:36; 5:17; 8:54). It was sometimes also in terms of prompting him to place himself in a vulnerable position in relation to others: for example, with the religious and civil authorities of his day (Luke 5:17, 21, 29–32; 6:6f; 11:53), and also with his own family and community (Luke 4:16, 28ff; 8:19f). Jesus also knew what it was to take risks with people's expectations (Luke 5:4; 7:36f). He faced the consequences of both speaking out (Luke 4:23f) and of remaining silent (Luke 23:9). He spoke of a way of life characterised by poverty, suffering and pain (Luke 6:20f); he taught in parables which illustrated the same (Luke 10:25f; 15:11f), and pointed to a child as an example of greatness (Luke 9:46–8). He emphasised the true cost of following his way (Luke 9:23; 14:27) and the demands of mission (Luke 9:3; 10:3; cf. 12:11), and witnessed both by his teaching and his example to the truth that 'all who exalt themselves will be humbled, and those who humble themselves will be exalted' (Luke 14:11; 18:14 cf. 22:26–7). In short, he lived out his self-emptying in a chosen vulnerability.

For all of this, he was dependent not only on his relationship, through the Spirit, with the Father – a relationship nurtured and maintained by a life of prayer – but also on his closest and most intimate circle of disciples. That is why the 'relational' approach of John Owen and those who, in our own day, have rediscovered the richness of a truly Trinitarian approach to theology really matters. The 'condescending God' in the person of his incarnate Son, Jesus Christ, establishes a relationship of love between himself and humanity which is faithful and true and ultimately costly. That costly vulnerability was made possible only because of the security of the relationships – with God and with his closest followers – in which he was set. Vulnerability is possible only in such a context.

It was prayer and the intimacy of community (human and divine) which freed the incarnate Son of God to so 'empty himself' and choose to be vulnerable to those around him. It is to these two areas of vulnerable living that we now turn.

> *Behold the father is his daughter's son,*
> *The bird that built the nest is hatched therein,*
> *The old of years an hour doth not outrun,*
> *Eternal life to live doth now begin,*
> *The Word is dumb, the mirth of heaven doth weep,*
> *Might feeble is, and force doth faintly creep.*[11]

NOTES

1. From 'My Lord's Love' in Eric Milner-White, *My God, My Glory* (SPCK, London, 1967).

2. 'The sign by which the shepherds are to recognise the Christchild is a paradoxical one and probably signals the humility of the divine condescension: God allows his Christ to be without outward splendour.' John Nolland, *Luke* (Dallas Texas, Word, 1989), p. 112.

3. *This . . . does not mean that every detail of his life is to be copied literally and directly in our life. Nevertheless, the problem then arises how – for example – the poverty, humiliation, persecution and the rest of Jesus' sufferings are to be imitated by us, if we cannot in fact copy the actual details . . . We shall have to be content with the two purely theoretical statements: first, the concrete life of Jesus is the final norm of our life, not to be judged by any higher norm; second, we cannot and may not simply copy Jesus, because it is precisely in our own situation that we must*

continue the life of Jesus in a new way ... (Karl Rahner, Meditations on Priestly
Life (London, Sheed & Ward, 1973))

4. For a particularly helpful discussion of this passage, see N. T. Wright, *The Climax
of the Covenant*, Chapter 4 'Jesus Christ is Lord' (Edinburgh, T & T Clark, 1991),
pp. 56–98.

5. Various suggestions have been made over the centuries to answer these questions,
and each has been shaped by the world-view of the time. For example, when the
early church struggled with the question of Christ's self-emptying, it was in the context
of a world where the thinking of the Greeks (especially Plato) was particularly
influential. To the Greek mind, it was inconceivable for the eternal and divine to
inhabit the changing and decaying environment of mortals. It is not surprising,
therefore, that the Fathers of the Church struggled over several centuries (and with
several swings of the pendulum) to reconcile the divinity and humanity of the
incarnate Son of God (for example, at the Councils of Nicea 325CE, Constantinople
381CE and Chalcedon 451CE). Their final if not entirely adequate solution was to
ascribe to the incarnate Son 'two natures in one person, without confusion, without
change, without division, without separation' (Chalcedon 451CE). Such an ascription
sounds strange to us because our understanding of person has been informed by the
developments of psychology over the past one hundred and fifty years. We tend to
think of 'person' in terms of 'personality', that is, in a limited way. When Chalcedon
spoke of the 'person' of the incarnate Son, it would have been understood to
encompass body, soul, will and centre of consciousness. Thus, for Chalcedon, the
'person' of the incarnate Son means the eternal Son of God who assumed a full and
complete human nature. It was not a case of 'either-or', but of 'both-and'. What is
important, however, is how that human personhood was expressed – and that is where
Christ's self-emptying becomes paramount.

6. *Church Dogmatics* IV. 1.59.1 p. 180 (Edinburgh, T & T Clark, 1956).

7. Barth is insistent that if the incarnate Son, as Jesus, ceases – in any way – to be
the eternal Son of God, then this has enormous implications for our understanding
of salvation:

> We cannot possibly understand or estimate [the Christological mystery] if we try
> to explain it by a self-limitation or de-divinisation of God in the unity of the Son
> of God with the man Jesus. If in Christ – even in the humiliated Christ born in a
> manger at Bethlehem, and crucified on the cross of Golgotha – God is not unchanged
> and wholly God, then everything that we may say about the reconciliation of the
> world made by God in this humiliated One is left hanging in the air. (Church
> Dogmatics IV. 1.59.1 p. 183 (Edinburgh, T & T Clark, 1956))

8. Charles Gore, who was one of the champions of Kenotic theory in Britain in the
early twentieth century, had suggested that the incarnate Son operated, as it were,
from two distinct centres of his being – one human and one divine. There is, however,
no legacy in Scripture for such a duality. Rather, Christ's human life was lived out of
a centre in the eternal Son of God (enhypostasia) and, as such, the eternal Son made
himself vulnerable to the struggles of humanity. For example, when we read that Jesus,
as Son of God, 'set his face to Jerusalem' or sweated blood in the Garden of Geth-

semane, it is not a question of whether it is God *or* humanity which is struggling – it is both!

9. Such an idea is also explored by Kenneth Bailey in *Finding the Lost: Cultural Keys to Luke 15* (St Louis, Concordia Publishing House, 1992) and Henri Nouwen in *Return of the Prodigal Son. A Story of Homecoming* (London, DLT, 1995), pp. 55–8.

10. In C. Schwöbel and C. Gunton (eds) *Persons, Divine and Human* (Edinburgh, T & T Clark, 1992).

11. Robert Southwell, 'The Nativity of Christ' in *The Faber Book of Religious Verse*, ed. Helen Gardner (London and Boston, Faber & Faber Ltd., 1972).

3

Living Vulnerability: Prayer

Each day a first day:
each day a life.
Each morning we must hold out the
chalice of our being
to receive,
to carry
and give back.
It must be held out empty – for the past must only be reflected
in its polish, its shape, its capacity . . .[1]

In Dag Hammarskjöld's image of the chalice there is a wonderful simplicity about a life lived for God. Such a life embraces our past but is not lessened by it. Indeed our past may increase our capacity to love and to be aware of our relationship with God. It is in our ability to lay ourselves open to God, to offer each day as an empty chalice, that we may be filled again, and may again give ourselves, by choice, to God.

In following a vulnerable Lord we follow one who is open to the Father, one who has been described as 'pure receptivity of the Father'.[2] It was in his relationship to the Father through the Spirit that Jesus was able to be obedient in love. So with us. If we want to give God anything at all then all we can give him is access to our life, whatever that life may be. Prayer is as simple and as demanding as that. A monk writes,

You think that loving God means giving him something? Give him access, that is all that he requires: for loving God means offering ourselves to the liberality of his love: it means letting him love us.[3]

In this chapter we attempt to explore what giving God access means in everyday life as we reflect on the prayer and life of Jesus. Each stage of his life marks a different aspect of prayer and in pondering those aspects it may be that our life of prayer can be enlightened and encouraged.

Birth

That God should choose to make himself vulnerable by becoming man in a baby is mystery beyond telling. There, in the stable, God reveals his 'kenosis' not in theological abstraction but in human flesh. There is in this 'hidden' birth a reflection of Jesus' teaching in Matthew 6 that we should give alms and should pray not in the full gaze of others but in the secret place. In Bethlehem God reveals himself in the secret place, the place of poverty. Here God empties himself to become man, here God fills himself with humanity. Here is God's prayer, his word spoken in silence.

There is much to ponder as we ponder this birth and the events that led up to Jesus' baptism and ministry, a pattern which is fore-shadowed by the early life of John the Baptist. For both Jesus and John their early lives are depicted as having a development which embraced spiritual as well as physical growth. For both of them, that growing takes place secretly (Luke 1:80, 2:40, 52). It is not surprising then to find later in Luke's gospel that Jesus teaches that the Kingdom of God is like mustard seed or yeast (Luke 13:18ff). The Kingdom, like the King, grows silently and hidden in the secret place until the time is right for its revelation.

If we wish to grow in God, if we desire to give him access, it is to this secret place that we need go. The 'secret place' in which Jesus bids us pray, the place which is hidden from public scrutiny, is the heart, that central place in us which God has made for himself and which alone can truly respond fully to God's coming. To enter that place, to seek God there, is to befriend silence and solitude.

In other words it is to learn to be alone with God, to have space for God and a place of meeting, like Moses' Tent of Meeting, to which to return. Silence and solitude are not just luxuries for a committed few. They are the very ground in which God places his seed and they are possible even in the midst of a busy life and a hectic schedule, for the silence is the silence of the heart and the solitude a trust in God beyond all else. To gain this inner silence and solitude it is, however, often necessary for us to risk at times entering a period of external silence when we can be alone with God. Lionel Blue writes,

It is good to steady yourself with silence. Eternity is all around you and is friendlier than you think. But you have to shut out the background noise outside you and inside you. Silence is not something to frighten you.[4]

Quite simply, we need space and time for God alone if he is to bring himself to birth in us, if he is to nurture us. The image of Bethlehem and of thirty years of hidden life is the image of that deep communion with God which happens when we allow him to touch us. 'The far-off event in Bethlehem is truly fulfilled and understood only when it becomes a *present* reality, enacted within ourselves, uniting us with God *now*.'[5]

Baptism

Grown now and become man, Jesus comes to John to be baptised and there receives his Father's call, his Father's blessing. There is no doubt, in this moment of glory (a moment which finds its echo in the Transfiguration and Gethsemane), that the relationship between Father and Son in the power of the Spirit is central to the giftedness of being emptied and being filled. At these moments of glory we hear an echo of Paul's 'therefore': '*therefore* God also highly exalted him' (Phil. 2:9).

The Baptism reminds us too of our own spiritual journey, our baptism into Christ, and of our need of the Holy Spirit. It reminds us that 'relationship' is the heart of prayer. Looking back to when Jesus was twelve, the clue was already there. When Mary and Joseph come, worried and distracted, searching for Jesus in the Temple, they find him in his Father's house. He is doing the one thing necessary.

It is enough for us to be in relationship with God.[6] For Jesus and for us that necessitates making the space and daring to believe that God loves us.

> *A woman came on Retreat unable to believe that God loved her. She was accustomed in the past to praying with a rosary so the Retreat conductor suggested that she recite a 'Rosary of Love',[7] saying 'My God, I love you' on each of the ten beads and then 'My God, I love you with all my heart' on the separate bead. She went round her rosary until she came to the Cross. There her words changed: 'My God, you love me.' Of her own instinct she went around the beads again . . . 'My God, you love me. My God, you love me. My God, you love me with all your heart.'*

Coming to the realisation of God's love was not spontaneous. She had been a Christian for some time and knew that God loved her as a fact. Now she knew by experience. Such an experience cannot be rushed. It is not something we can make happen at a time which suits us but we can be open and receptive, vulnerable to God's moment when it comes. To know ourselves as 'loved sinners' and in relationship with God means that we can be relaxed in our prayer, content to be silent and still, to speak of our concerns and cares or to gently sing God's praise. What it means to be a loved sinner is caught graphically by Joachim Jeremias as he tries to summarise the Sermon on the Mount:

You are forgiven: you are the child of God; you belong to his Kingdom. The sun of righteousness has risen over your life. You no longer belong to yourself; rather you belong to the city of God, the light of which shines in the darkness. Now you may also experience it: out of the thankfulness of a redeemed child of God a new life is growing.[8]

Desert

St Luke begins his account of the desert and his account of Jesus' public ministry with similar phrases. Jesus was 'full of the Holy Spirit' (4:1), 'filled with the power of the Holy Spirit' (4:14). Like the chalice

Jesus lifts himself to the Father and is filled, inebriated with God's Spirit, but is led by that Spirit into the wilderness.

It is not surprising that many people shy away from silence and from the desert places for to enter silence and space is to confront ourselves and our fears. In fact although the desert invites us to face our fears, the Spirit leads us into our wilderness not to destroy us but to strengthen us. There is a wonderful image in Luke 22:31 when Jesus says to Peter,

Simon, Simon, listen! Satan has demanded to sift all of you like wheat but I have prayed for you that your own faith may not fail; and you, once you have turned back, strengthen your brothers.

God needs to build up our spiritual strength and he does so in the wilderness. There we will confront the reality of ourselves and will need to let go of illusions. There we will find ourselves, with Jesus, calling on God, refuting all that is false with the reality of God's love. There we will learn to be faithful.

> *A young man at the beginning of his Christian journey was surprised when his initial joy and enthusiasm gave way to a period of dryness and pain. He turned to a friend for help. The friend explained the pattern of Jesus, baptism giving way to wilderness and how God promises to teach each one of us his way of discipleship. Years later the man's wife entered a period of depression. Looking back he could see how God had carried him through his 'wilderness' and, in a deeper way, he was enabled to be there for his wife while she traversed hers.*

The wilderness is the place too where we come to a deeper understanding not only of our own reality but also of God.[9] It is, paradoxically, a time of affirmation not despite, but because of, the stripping away of all that is false. It is not enough for followers of Christ to be clean on the outside.[10] We have to dare to allow God to reveal our inner darkness in order that he may heal us. The wilderness place will be the place where we, like Peter, need to be faithful in prayer and steadfast in love although it may feel to us that nothing is happening, even that no one is listening (Luke 8:15, 21:19).

Our prayer may become no more than sitting silently before God for the allotted time. To sit still in the desert and still to be receptive is to be truly vulnerable and it is to follow Christ. It is also to learn the art of waiting, which is itself a large part of prayer.[11]

Teaching and Preaching

> The Spirit of the Lord is upon me,
>> because he has anointed me
>>> to bring good news to the poor.
> He has sent me to proclaim release to
>> the captives
>> and recovery of sight to the blind,
>>> to let the oppressed go free,
> to proclaim the year of the Lord's favour. (Luke 4:18–19)

Prayer and life go together. It may even be said that our life is our prayer. So Jesus' life, filled with the Holy Spirit, reveals his deep prayer of self giving to the Father by being a life of self giving to others. His prayer and life are integral to each other. He neither pursues the inner journey to the exclusion of the outer, nor so busies himself being available to others that he loses his own space where the inner life can be nurtured.

In an age where the hunger for something new is apparent, where people so easily follow one spiritual bandwagon and then another, it is good to ponder the character of Zechariah. Here is a man who reveals vulnerability before God. He stands in the 'sanctuary of the Lord' because he was on duty and because he had been chosen by lot (Luke 1:8–9). In other words he might just have been going through the motions. Perhaps the last thing he expected was an experience of God, let alone an angel. No wonder he was terrified, but it is to this man going about his duty, this man who did not easily believe God's word, that a son, John, was born. The image of Zechariah doing what is required of him is of practical service rather than spiritual hunger. God uses such vulnerability to bring about his will. Often it is when we feel least 'spiritual' but are still faithfully doing what is required that God calls us again, draws us deeper into fellowship with himself. The gift of perseverance, patience and steadfastness is often the gift that carries us through. Michael Ramsey draws us to see the work of the Spirit in this too:

Where exciting charismata are seen, there is the Spirit, but where hard work is done with cheerful and unexciting perseverance, where sorrow and pain are borne with quiet fortitude, where scholars pursue the truth with patience, where contemplatives serve us all by praying with a love beyond our experience, here too is the Holy Spirit, here too is the charismatic Christ.[12]

The real test of our lives is not the intensity of our religious experience but the reality of our love, and love makes us vulnerable to hard unrewarding work. It implies a commitment to truth, a willingness to offer patient care, the development of an empathy which allows another to express their frailty and find acceptance, and a following of the kenosis of Christ in being ourselves emptied. As Jesus found too in this early visit to Nazareth at the beginning of his ministry, such practical honest love may not be the way to easy popularity (Luke 4:29).

O Lord let me feel at one with myself. Let me perform a thousand daily tasks with love, but let every one spring from a greater central core of devotion and love.[13]

Transfiguration

We have seen in Chapter 2 that the work of the Holy Spirit in relating is vital – both in terms of relationship with the Father and in terms of relationships with other human beings. We may, as we consider contemplative prayer, recognise too that it is in the power of the Holy Spirit that we are set free into all truth (John 8:31). How can this be? The pursuit of truth is no less than the search for God who alone is true. Those who begin that search look for the truth incarnate in each person and for the God-given 'essence' which lies at the heart of every part of creation. In being open for that truth we make ourselves vulnerable in the extreme; for truth cannot be narrowly defined but involves a radical openness to reality wherever it is found, in the belief that God is in all that he has made. To discover that truth means to be ready to see and to look with a steady gaze until the object of our gaze reveals itself.

There is a readiness to see and there is a committed looking. We may call the first 'purity of heart' and the other 'contemplation'. It is the pure in heart, those open to reality, those vulnerable to the liberality of God's love, who will see God and it is those who dare to look attentively who will find him in the strangest places – sometimes in the heights of joy and at other times in the deepest pain.

The story of the Transfiguration reveals Jesus again filled with the Holy Spirit and again the voice speaks, 'This is my Son, my chosen, listen to him!' (Luke 9:35). Here Jesus is not alone but is surrounded by a circle of intimacy – the intimacy of Elijah and Moses but also of human company, Peter, James and John. Revelation is often so. It often takes place not in isolation but in encounter. As Jesus encounters Elijah and Moses so there is a clarity of listening to the voice. The disciples reveal the contemplative stance of watching (despite being 'weighed down by sleep'!) and listening. They see Jesus transfigured but after the encounter they see Jesus alone. How often that happens. When we have a moment of intimacy with God we can seldom replay it – a piece of music which somehow touched our soul may at second listening be only music, the landscape which moved us to tears may become just fields. Revelation is God's gift and not at our disposal.

The Transfiguration also reveals to us this supreme relationship between Jesus and the Father. Jesus gives the Father full access. On the mountain Jesus, alone, is said to be praying. The disciples watch and listen. It is a powerful reminder that all prayer is Jesus' prayer. By giving God access we may allow Jesus to pray in us.

It is in this contemplation of all that is, and in this gazing at God, that we are more and more transformed into his likeness. This is a way of living prayer which is not for a select few but is a possibility for many. It is not a negative withdrawal from life, but rather entering life at a deeper level. Etty Hillesum, a Dutch Jew influenced by Christian understanding, writes,

However, one must keep in touch with the real world and know one's place in it. To live fully, outwardly and inwardly, not to ignore external reality for the sake of the inner life, or the reverse – that's quite a task.[14]

And in writing of her, J. G. Gaarlandt says,

Her mysticism led her not into solitary contemplation but squarely back into the world of action. Her vision had nothing to do with escape or self-deception, and everything to do with a hard-won, steady and whole perception of reality. Her God, in a sense, resides in her own capacity to see the truth, to bear it and find consolation in it.[15]

It is in this capacity to reflect on the whole of life that we not only have the experience of life but may begin to grasp its meaning.

Gethsemane and Passion

If the Transfiguration sees Jesus bathed in light then Gethsemane sees him in the darkest place and yet still drawn to his vocation of being fully accessible to the Father. This aspect of prayer, the encounter with darkness, is all too real. We encounter not only our own darkness but that of others. We may, too, find ourselves consciously carrying some of the darkness of the world. There is a deep reality about this encounter and carrying which is a reality of prayer. This is part of our offering to God, to share Christ's passion and suffering.

It is part of a life of chosen vulnerability. Again it is not just the path of a few super-spiritual people. It is part of the path for most people who seek to pray.[16] Jesus tells his disciples about it often (e.g. Luke 21:16ff).

Preaching from the text 'You will be hated by all', a preacher left his congregation disinterested and bored. Then his tone changed, people listened. For a few minutes he let go of the masks, stopped the platitudes and the borrowed expressions of religious rectitude, and spoke from his heart. Speaking about the rejection that Christians suffer, he suggested that there were several layers – the understandable rejection by the world, the rejection which is harder to bear which comes from friends and family, but worse still was the rejection that comes from within one's heart, the undermining struggle to actually do what you believe God is calling you to do. The congregation, looking at the preacher, could see he was speaking his truth and theirs. These layers of rejection and darkness are common to all of us.

The task is not to ignore them nor be overwhelmed by them but to be the place where darkness can be touched by the overwhelming love of God so that in us and through us there may be healing. To consent to be in that place is to say 'Yes' to God at a deep level. It is to consent to allowing Christ to be born in us, to pray in us and to minister through us to others.

This 'Yes', this 'Fiat', lies at the heart of our vulnerability. It is our acceptance of God's will as supreme. So Mary says 'Fiat': 'Let it be to me according to your word' (Luke 1:38). It is the 'Yes' which embraces the whole of our being, the 'Yes' which is the birth of God's Word again and again in our soul. To allow God's living and active word to pierce us totally until 'it divides soul from spirit, joints from marrow' (Heb. 4:12), to be rendered 'naked and laid bare' to his eyes (Heb. 4:13), is to allow our very core to be touched and changed by God. This is the efficacy of the divine word in our inmost depths. It is, says Jesus, when we continue in his word that we are truly his disciples (John 8:31). To say 'Yes' to God is to consent to be vulnerable to God and it is to put ourselves under his word.

Resurrection

> *The man sat in the church. It was Easter morning and he was meant to feel joyous. Christ has risen! Alleluia! Instead he felt anxious and afraid. Life had been busy. Work was getting difficult. Maybe he would be made redundant. How could he tell his wife, recently become a mother? Easter joy seemed remote.*

So often Easter comes, like revelation, not at our bidding, not when the calendar says it should, but rather at God's time.

> *A man on retreat had prayed through the whole of Jesus' life. Having been through the Passion there was some anticipation of waking up to pray with the scriptures and to begin to pray through*

the Easter story. Morning came and he began to pray. His prayer,
like the tomb, was empty. There was little joy.

It was only later, on reflection, that he remembered a persistent
thought that had come to him in the night about his job. He knew
he felt guilty about leaving his job, as though he was letting
everyone down. In the night he had heard some words from Psalm
81: 'I have eased your shoulder of the burden.' Taking those to
prayer filled the emptiness with a sense of peace, of quiet joy. The
resurrection was no longer an event of two hundred years ago. It
impinged on the here and now, on the circumstances of his life.
He was being set free.

It is when we are vulnerable enough to carry our cross daily (Luke
9:23) that we can truly be used in the ministry of Christ for it is then
that we will be ready for the resurrection to break out in the everyday.

Throughout Luke's gospel there are 'resurrections' – the child given
to the childless Zechariah and Anna, the restoration of the son of
the widow of Nain (7:11ff), for example. In fact Chapter 7 is full
of such incidents, not only that of the widow's son but the centurion's
daughter and in a different way the woman who comes to the table
where Jesus eats (Luke 7:36ff). For her the salvation of the passion,
death and resurrection is wrought by this meeting with Jesus. Quite
simply she gives him access and he fills her, forgiving her and loving
her into new life.

Resurrection of this kind in the daily events of life can so easily
go unnoticed while we look for the more dramatic. Quiet reflection
can often reveal to us how God has been moving us on, how he has
revealed himself through the everyday events of life, how he has said
'Yes' to us. It is in this relationship of love which involves mutual
consent that the work of the incarnation goes forward.

A group of children were asked how they would describe a saint.
One lad, his eyes wandering round the building and looking at the
stained glass windows, suggested 'A saint is someone that the light
shines through.'

It is when we are prepared for the light of the resurrection to shine through us, when we allow God to shine through our dark-stained glass as well as through the golden and the clear, that the whole of our being can be used in God's service. In him we will find our own resurrection, that we are loved and forgiven. In him we find too that, like Peter, being loved and forgiven means also to be commissioned to love others. It is in this sense of abandonment that we may follow a Lord who 'emptied himself'.

The Kenosis of Prayer

There are some beautiful words in the Methodist Covenant service which capture this need to be open to whatever God will do. They form a prayer:

I am no longer my own, but yours. Put me to what you will, rank me with whom you will; put me to doing, put me to suffering; let me be employed for you or laid aside for you, exalted for you or brought low for you; let me be full, let me be empty; let me have all things, let me have nothing; I freely and wholeheartedly yield all things to your pleasure and disposal. And now, glorious and blessed God, Father, Son and Holy Spirit, you are mine and I am yours. So be it. And the covenant now made on earth, let it be ratified in heaven. Amen. (The Methodist Service Book)

To pray these words is to follow a tradition of self-abandonment to God which finds its origin in the biblical words of self-gift, 'Here I am', and primarily in Christ himself. The image is clear. It is almost as simple as having an empty glass and waiting for God to pour the water. Experience, though, is not quite like that. We live with a past and with our present needs and desires. It is not easy to be empty. This chapter began with a quotation from Dag Hammarskjöld which draws another image in which all our past and present is used to shape the vessel. The vessel is still to be empty but the vessel itself embraces all our experience. This is the true emptiness we offer: not an emptiness which ignores our true selves but one which embraces our true selves; an emptiness which has allowed God to use our past pains and hurts, and our desire for him, to carve out a space in us capable of holding God himself, a space, as the tradition has it, *capax Dei* – capable of holding God.

God calls us to be this place not only to be empty but also to be full. This too demands a transparency to God, a contemplative stance of listening and watching. It may be a matter of seeing through the beauty of nature and seeing the beauty of God, or of listening to beautiful music and hearing the heart-rending harmony of God, or of looking at someone we love and seeing God's love, or seeing in the person of the distressed and the needy the distressed and needy Christ. To see life in this way is to be filled with love and with compassion. The fullness as well as the emptiness is part of the transparency, part of the vulnerability. Above all it is about gazing at God for his sake alone.

This is the point of surrender, the daily abandonment to God. If the ministry of the church truly is the ministry of Christ then it is the daily prayer of those who minister in Christ's name that they do not obstruct his ministry but may be used in it. It is a prayer which at times will be an act of will and at other times the words of those who know themselves in love. But it is this prayer, however it is expressed, which lies at the heart of vulnerability in ministry. The vulnerability is primarily a vulnerability towards God, a willingness to be wounded by love, human and divine, and not to protect oneself from the consequences.

It is a surrender which stems from being in love with God. It is the surrender which we see within the Godhead:

Within himself, God is the mutual offering of Person to Person. How would we hope to become like him in any way, if we are not equally open with all our being to an unlimited reciprocal gift?[17]

It is the surrender of a loving Son to a loving Father, a surrender expressed in swaddling bands, in nappies and feet-drying towels, in nails and thorns, in empty tombs and air full of praise.

In this chapter we have suggested that the way of vulnerability is the way of prayer. Such prayer involves the willingness to allow the life of Christ to be revealed through our life. It means that we will discover that at different stages in our life we see ourselves at one with Christ in his crucifixion and at another stage at one with him in his resurrection or in his birth or at some other stage. To be willing is to give our consent not only to God but to the reality of our own self, in order that we may be wholly transparent to God. Dag Hammarskjöld puts it this way:

To say Yes to life is at one and the same time to say Yes to oneself. . . Yes – even to that element in one which is most unwilling to let itself be transformed from a temptation into a strength.[18]

The way of vulnerability is the way of God. The choice, though, is ours.

> *It comes from the depth of my being,*
> *this 'Yes' to God.*
> *It tears me to pieces and makes me whole.*
> *It yearns in my deepest desire,*
> *and gives birth to the deepest*
> > *fresh-born,*
> > > *frisson,*
> > > > *fun –*
> *God's joy.*
> *It finds a deep, pot-bellied*
> > *laughing echo –*
> *a God who understands*
>
> *And listening to*
> > *the silence of my*
> > > *'Yes'*
> *the sound of God's joy overwhelms*
> *though the whisper on*
> *God's breath is so gentle.*
>
> *Yes, he says. Yes.*[19]

NOTES
1. Dag Hammarskjöld, *Markings* (London, Faber & Faber, 1964), p. 127.
2. A Carthusian, *The Wound of Love* (London, DLT, 1994), p. 55.

3. A Monk, *The Hermitage Within* (London, DLT, 1977).

4. Lionel Blue, *Here and Hereafter* (London, Collins, 1988).

5. Cyprian Smith, *The Way of Paradox* (London, DLT, 1987), p. 77.

6. See Mary and Martha (Luke 10:38–42).

7. The 'Rosary of Love' is mentioned in George Gorree, *Memories of Charles de Foucauld* (London, Burns Oates and Washbourne Ltd, 1938).

8. Joachim Jeremias, *The Sermon of the Mount* (London, The Athlone Press, 1961), p. 32.

9. See also Chapter 9 on 'Trust'.

10. See Luke 11:38.

11. See Chapter 7.

12. Owen Chadwick, *Michael Ramsey* (Oxford, Clarendon Press, 1990), p. 217.

13. Etty Hillesum, *An Interrupted Life* (New York, Washington Square Press, 1985), p. 71.

14. ibid.

15. ibid, Introduction.

16. For example, see William Johnston, *Being in Love* (London, Fount Paperbacks, 1989), p. 120. ' . . . the dark night is the royal road to God. It is not the soteric road of a few privileged mystics; it is the road of every human being who approaches a God of inaccessible light or darkness.'

17. Carthusian, p. 40.

18. Hammarskjöld, p. 89.

19. Ivan Mann.

4

Living Vulnerability:
Community

Those who were sensitive to these things could tell that there was something wrong. They asked if she was okay. To some, she simply said she was over-tired. To others, she admitted that there was a problem: she couldn't say what it was, but would they pray? There was only one person in the community who knew the whole story, and only two others anywhere in the world . . .

In Chapter 3, we began to explore the place of prayer as one of vulnerability before God, as the place of abandoning our masks before him and of allowing ourselves to be loved, healed, forgiven and commissioned as his co-workers in vulnerable love. We saw how, for Christ, times of quiet withdrawal for prayer both strengthened and affirmed his relationship with the Father and the Spirit (cf. Luke 4:42; 5:1–2, 16; 9:98), and allowed the scars of human misunderstanding and pain to be healed (cf. Luke 6:12 following on from 6:1–11!).

In this chapter, we turn to look at our vulnerability before other people. For it is one thing to acknowledge that God sees through our masks and yet loves us; it is another to allow others (or even ourselves) to see through those masks *and believe that we might still be loved.* The hermit or the recluse may have the freedom to be vulnerable before God and themselves alone. Those who exercise leadership live, by virtue of that leadership, as part of a community. They relate not only to God in prayer, but also to those amongst whom they are set and whom they seek to serve. Whether, and with whom, to be vulnerable thus becomes a matter for discernment, a matter of choice. For just as we can choose not to acknowledge our vulnerability before God, so we can choose not to acknowledge our vulnerability before members of the communities of which we are a part. The woman in the example at the beginning of this chapter had exercised that choice: although others were aware that something was wrong (for pain often permeates even the masks we wear), only one person in the community knew the whole story. For her, there were *circles of intimacy* and *degrees of disclosure*: for one member of the community, the mask had been removed; for others it remained securely in place.

This chapter aims to do three things. Firstly, to look at the vulnerability of the incarnate Son within the communities to which he belonged, as expressed in the gospel of Luke. Secondly, to look at a number of situations in which one member of a community chose to be vulnerable before the others, and to discuss whether the disclosure which took place was necessary or appropriate. Thirdly, in the light of contemporary culture, to explore the mask as both a positive and a negative image, and to suggest that sometimes it is more costly to wear a mask than it is to dispense with it.

Jesus Christ 'in community'

It is impossible to speak of the communities within which the incarnate Son operated, without acknowledging (as we intimated in Chapter 2) the divine community within which he already existed and to which, in his incarnation, he did not cease to belong. For God's very being, his life as Trinity, is constituted in his 'being-in-communion'.[1] God *is* who he is only because of the relational community of love *which* he is. Within that community of love, there is a dynamic unity of mutual indwelling (perichoresis), where Father, Son and Spirit are 'fully known'. There are no masks either within the Trinity, nor anything 'behind' God as he reveals himself to humanity: who he is in himself, *he is* – in the incarnation of Jesus Christ – *to humanity*.

Jesus knew what it was to live within the perfect divine community which is God. Yet he chose to become vulnerable to the imperfections of human communities, so as ultimately to redeem them and restore them to perfect communion with the Father in heaven (Rev. 21:3, 7). No human community, this side of eternity, can ever 'match' that community of love within which the Son continually dwells. Nevertheless, in his incarnation, Jesus demonstrated a way of vulnerable living in community, from which humanity may learn.

Jesus did not relate to all with whom he came into contact in precisely the same way. Prompted, in his humanity, by the Holy Spirit, he discerned the appropriate way to speak and to be with each person or group with whom he came into contact. In Luke's gospel, we see him not only exercising extraordinary authority and power, as in the casting out of demons (Luke 4:36) or the stilling of the storm (Luke 8:22ff), but also choosing to place himself in the firing line of both the religious and civil authorities (Luke 5:17, 21, 29–32; 6:6f; 11:53) and his own family and community (Luke 4:16, 28ff; 8:19f). This greatness and chosen vulnerability are, perhaps, thrown into sharpest relief at what might be described as the 'turning points' in his life and ministry, that is, in his birth, baptism, temptations, transfiguration and passion. At these key moments, we can recognise his dependence on both the divine and human communities: on his Father, through the Spirit, and on his human circle of disciples, a circle which, interestingly, is not constant, but which develops and changes over the years.

In Chapter 2 we pointed out the paradoxes of the incarnation: the juxtaposition of the ordinary and the extraordinary, of richness and poverty thrown together in the birth of the Bethlehem-child. Little is said of Jesus' childhood, although his kinship community would surely have been of great significance as he grew (see Luke 2:40, 51–52). Nevertheless, his primary relationship – even at this early stage – was with his heavenly Father (Luke 2:49), and, as the gospel unfolds, his kinship relationships give way to those he had with his close followers (Luke 8:19–21). Friendships became more significant than family.

Great crowds flocked to see and hear Jesus during the early part of his ministry (Luke 4:42; 5:1; 6:17) as he taught and healed in the power of the Spirit. Gradually, however, both his teaching *and his relating* became more intimately focused: to the disciples (Luke 6:20; 8:9), then the twelve (Luke 6:12–16; 9:1), and then to the three – Peter,

James and John (Luke 8:51; 9:28; 22:8). The teaching and insight granted to each group varied (Luke 8:9–10; 10:22–4), as did the extent to which Jesus revealed his own feelings and needs. At times he was frustrated, stressed and impatient with the crowds (Luke 12:49–50); at other times, and in the face of suffering, he longed for intimacy, reassurance and support from his friends (Luke 22:14–15, 39f). At *all* times he was dependent on his heavenly Father.

We see this interdependence, both human and divine, most clearly, perhaps, in the account of the Transfiguration (Luke 9:28–36). Just over a week earlier, Jesus had spoken openly to his disciples about his impending passion and death (Luke 9:21–2). He had sought reassurance from them concerning his identity: 'Who do the crowds say that I am?' (Luke 9:18). At his transfiguration he received the full affirmation of his heavenly Father (with echoes of his baptism, and again in the context of prayer) in the presence of the intimate circle of Peter, James and John: 'This is my Son, my Chosen: listen to him!' (Luke 9:35). In his humanity, Jesus needed support and assurance both from his Father, through the Holy Spirit, *and from those closest to him.* He could not have demonstrated his frustration and hesitations to everybody; he could not – at this stage – have been revealed in glory to any but those most closely associated with him, for even they did not understand the significance of what they had seen and heard until after the events of the passion and resurrection (Luke 9:36). In his humanity, Jesus needed the intimacy of human community as well as that which was always his by virtue of his divinity.

But how did Jesus know *what* to disclose and *with whom*? How did he discern what was appropriate with one person or group and not with another? How did he know when and how to be vulnerable? The answer to those questions is the same as we have already suggested in Chapter 2. For he was dependent, in his humanity, on the power, strength and guiding of the Spirit, and on his relationship of love with his heavenly Father mediated by that same Spirit and maintained through the intimacy of his life of prayer.

Those same resources are available to all who are leaders in the Christian community today. Relationship with the Father, through the Son, by the Holy Spirit – a relationship nurtured by a life of prayer – continues to be the foundation upon which those in leadership may rest as they seek to discern when, with whom, and how they may choose to be vulnerable in the communities in which they live and work.

Henri Nouwen discovered this possibility afresh when he left the world of academia to become a member of a L'Arche community in Toronto. He writes:

After twenty-five years of priesthood, I found myself praying poorly, living somewhat isolated from other people, and very much preoccupied with burning issues... So I moved from Harvard to L'Arche, from the best and the brightest, wanting to rule the world, to men and women who had few or no words and were considered, at best, marginal to the needs of society... Christian leaders... must be rooted in the permanent, intimate relationship with the incarnate Word, Jesus, and they need to find there the source for their words, advice, guidance. Through the discipline of contemplative prayer, Christian leaders have to learn to listen again and again to the voice of love and to find there the wisdom and courage to address whatever issue presents itself to them... I am convinced that priests and ministers... need a truly safe place for themselves... where they can share their deep pain and struggles with people who... can guide them ever deeper into the mystery of God's love. I, personally, have been fortunate in having found such a place in L'Arche, with a group of friends who pay attention to my own often-hidden pains and keep me faithful to my vocation by their gentle criticisms and loving support.[2]

There can be no hard and fast rules about when it is right to be vulnerable or when it is appropriate to remove the mask. What is clear, however, is that even in his vulnerability Jesus always acted or spoke in ways which demonstrated his overwhelming love for those to whom he ministered. When he allowed his feet to be washed by the tears of a prostitute and dried with hair (Luke 7:36ff), he knew he would reap condemnation from those around him (Luke 7:39, 49); but neither did he fight shy of speaking out his own condemnation of the inadequate hospitality of his host, Simon the Pharisee. He made himself vulnerable to both – to the woman by allowing her to minister to him, to Simon with his cutting criticism (Luke 7:41ff). It was the Spirit who prompted Jesus to act and speak as he did (Luke 7:39–40). Jesus did not deal with people as 'generalities' or 'types'; he dealt with them and loved them as *particular persons*, as those uniquely created and uniquely loved by his heavenly Father. Each one mattered, and each was treated appropriately, whatever the risk to his own reputation.

The example of Jesus, then, is of a leader rooted in a life of prayer, who related to different people in different ways, according to the prompting of the Holy Spirit. Within some circles of intimacy, he allowed his vulnerability to be seen. Within other contexts, he hid it. To the crowds, he was the charismatic teacher and healer; to the religious authorities, he was both a threat and a charlatan; to his closest friends, he was someone who knew what it was to feel under pressure, to feel alone, sad and – in his humanity – unsure of the way ahead. His is an example with which we can identify as we move on to consider whether 'disclosure' within *our* communities, and the vulnerability it so often brings in its wake, is necessary or appropriate.

The Community's Experience: Disclosure and Vulnerability

Disclosure always carries risk. To speak or demonstrate our truth to another person or within a community (as well as being the 'stuff' of which communities are made) always risks rejection, pain and misunderstanding. In any community, every member is affected by the words, the actions and the very presence of every other. With every exchange, every interaction, the community takes risks with itself, and makes itself vulnerable within itself. Such is the pain and joy of human relating. Nevertheless, against this background of what we might describe as 'vulnerability by default', members of any community, however large or small – family, household, congregation, work colleagues, religious or educational establishment – may choose to make their needs, weaknesses and feelings more explicit. The extent to which they do so (the *degree of disclosure*) will be dependent upon their security of relationship with God and with those around them. For 'safe' disclosure is dependent on trust in a context of love. Disclosure outside of such a relational context not only carries enormous risk, but may ultimately be destructive. The following examples may help to illustrate what we mean.

A group of students decided to share a house during their second and final years at university. Although they were on different courses, they all knew each other a little through their involvement in the university's Christian Union, and the local church. They agreed to commit themselves not only to the financial and practical responsibilities of renting the property and living together, but also to offering one another mutual support and regularly meeting to share and pray together.

Things went well for a few months. Gradually, however, one member of the group became resentful of the fact that others were not 'pulling their weight' with the practical tasks of washing up, cooking and cleaning. She decided to risk speaking to the others about this when they next met.

When she did, the other members of the household listened, and began to understand why she had been so preoccupied. There followed an exchange of similar frustrations amongst the group, which led not only to greater understanding, but to a deepening of friendship, trust and commitment. It also meant that it was easier, on later occasions, for the students to speak openly about their concerns without resentment building up in the same way.

A deacon, serving his title in a clergy team, found his relationship with one of the team vicars to be particularly trying. They were of very different personalities: the deacon organised, efficient and conscientious; the team vicar, a very caring and excellent pastor, with a very different style of working.

As the deacon's time for his ordination as priest drew near, he felt more and more angry towards his colleague and found it increasingly difficult to be loyal to him both within the clergy team and even with members of the congregation. Although he was the most junior member of the team, the deacon (in consultation with the team rector) decided to 'speak his truth' to his colleague, and ask for help in dealing with his anger and frustration.

The team vicar listened and was able to speak openly, for the first time, about some of his own difficulties with working in the team. Although their fundamental differences remained, they were enabled to acknowledge them and – potentially – deal with difficulties and misunderstandings as they arose. What was most significant for the deacon was that he felt he could go forward for ordination as priest without the weight of this unsatisfactory situation on his shoulders.

Two couples in leadership in a local congregation met together regularly to support each other and to pray for the work of the church in their area. They became very close, sharing not only their concerns for those amongst whom they worked but also more personal matters relating to their own marriages and families.

An opportunity arose for the wife of one couple and the husband of the other couple to go on an overseas visit with a group from the congregation. During their time away, they continued to share closely, as they would have done with their respective partners present.

On returning from the visit overseas, the woman who had been away shared with the foursome the increasing depth of feeling she held towards the husband of the other couple. Although the attraction was not mutual, she felt it was important to be 'open' about those feelings with the other three rather than to hide them from them.

The others were shocked by what she shared, and considerable turmoil followed as they tried to 'work through' the implications of what had been said. The long-term result was a strengthening of both sets of relationships, but not without considerable pain and misunderstanding on the way.

A Roman Catholic bishop tendered his resignation in the wake of the revelation by a national tabloid newspaper of his admission to a sexual liaison with a divorced woman, and suggestions that he had previously fathered another woman's child. The effect of his admission was felt not only by his own family and immediate community but across the world-wide Roman Catholic Church. The general public failed to cope with such an admission of failure from so senior a church leader: someone charged with the pastoral care of others should be morally above reproach. The media presented and encouraged an unsympathetic appraisal of the bishop's situation; the individual and the Church were scarred.

The four examples above illustrate a range of situations in which disclosures were made, and people became vulnerable as a result. In the brief discussion which follows, we shall not only look at the 'effects' of disclosure but also ask the underlying question: was the disclosure necessary and appropriate?

Whether a particular disclosure is necessary or appropriate will depend on the particular perspective of the parties involved. For whilst those making the disclosure may feel it is necessary, those associated with them may think differently. In the first example the female student had obviously reached a level of frustration with her peers which was affecting how she related to them. It was, in her judgement, necessary to speak out, although it may be that the other members of the household could have gone on functioning without the need for such a 'clearing of the air'. Similarly, it was necessary for the deacon to speak to his colleague *before* his ordination as priest. The team vicar may well have been able to continue without the need to 'sort things out' although clearly this may have precipitated further gossip and disloyalty within the clergy team and amongst the wider congregation.

In the third example the question of whether disclosure was necessary is less clearly answered. The woman obviously *felt* it was necessary and could not, with integrity, continue in such a closeness of relationship as couples, without admitting the depth of her feelings. On the other hand, it is questionable whether the other three people really *needed* to know. The woman might well have been wiser to share and work through her feelings, in confidence, with somebody 'outside' the situation.

In the last example the disclosure was made by a third party, with or without the bishop's permission. A cynic might suggest that such a disclosure was necessary both to boost the income of the divorcee, and the tabloid paper during a 'quiet' week! There are those who would argue that the public has a right to know about the failings of public figures; others would suggest that such a public display does little to enhance the life of a community or nation, and is best dealt with away from the public gaze.

Discussing disclosure and the vulnerability it brought in each of our examples, therefore, reveals the fact that discerning its necessity or appropriateness is not always straightforward. Human motivation and the prompting of the Holy Spirit are not always easily distinguished. The student wanted to deal with a frustrating situation but, at a deeper level, she was probably seeking greater mutual commitment and sensitivity between members of the household. The deacon too was dealing with anger and frustration with his colleague, on the surface, but at a deeper level he could not face his ordination when he felt so 'out of sorts' with him. In each of these situations, it would seem that *human* motivation and *spiritual* prompting worked together.

Sometimes, however, there is a tension between the two, and human motivation can often be the most persuasive. It is easy to convince ourselves that the 'unexpected' is of God! In such instances, discernment is still vital. (On the other hand, it is far harder to act on the prompting of the Holy Spirit, when our *human* instinct is to run a mile!) In the third example the woman's motivation was an honourable one: she sought an 'openness' in her relating to the others. Yet, in the light of the shock and confusion which it evoked, her disclosure was perhaps misguided, and not of the Spirit's prompting. In the case of the bishop the *human* motivation appears to have been the public disgrace of a senior church leader, ostensibly because 'people have the right to know' but more likely in the pursuit of scandal and increased sales. It may well have enabled people to recognise that 'bishops are human too' and even released the bishop from the continuing need to cover up his former misdemeanours; nevertheless, it provoked a wave of shock, negative criticism and disdain towards the Church, and considerable pain and shame for all involved as the bishop became the latest scapegoat for the public need to 'blame'. Thus the appropriateness of a disclosure can often only be assessed in the light of its effects.

When people risk 'speaking their truth', disclosing something of who they are behind the mask, they may illumine, challenge and affirm or they may, equally, undermine. Often disclosure will bring growth and release, both for those who make themselves vulnerable by speaking and for those to whom they speak. The very willingness of one person to remove the mask is the catalyst which frees others to do the same. Yet often, disclosure is accompanied by pain, abuse, misunderstanding or even rejection. Sometimes (perhaps *always*, if we would but admit it) there is a mixture of pain *and* growth. For even when a disclosure is unwise, or damaging, it is not beyond redemption if those involved are willing to seek it. In the case of the leadership couples love and forgiveness prevailed *even through the pain* and their relationships were strengthened and enriched.

It will be clear from our discussion that disclosure – the active choice to become vulnerable by word or deed – is a delicate issue. What is, perhaps, most striking about the examples we have offered is the difference between the first three and the last. In the former, the disclosure took place *in a relational context*. It was that which made 'safe' disclosure possible, and it was the trust and love already existing within those relationships which allowed those involved to work through the outcomes. Indeed, the depth of the relationship was, in some sense, in proportion to the amount of pain which had to be borne.

In the final example, however, things were different. It is debatable whether the disclosures made by the tabloid press were the bishop's choice – even if he had admitted that they were true. He seems, rather, to have been a victim of the media; his was not a chosen vulnerability. Equally significant, in this example, is the complete lack of a relational context for disclosure. Here, the degree of disclosure was out of all proportion to the *circle of intimacy* (a misnomer in this case, if ever there was one!) amongst whom that disclosure was made.

The vulnerability of disclosure, and the pain and growth it can bring, is part of the community's experience. It was, as we have seen, part of Jesus' human experience. He did not hesitate to 'speak his truth' although the degree to which he disclosed that truth depended upon the circle of intimacy within which he happened to be. For him, prayer and relationship were key: relationship with the Father, through the Spirit, and relationship with his closest followers. Even for him, that relational context mattered and he was enabled, by the Holy Spirit, to discern an appropriate degree of disclosure – an appropriate vulnerability – for each person, in each set of circumstances, *whatever the outcome might be*. That was what it meant for him to live vulnerably in community. That is what it may mean for those who choose to follow him today.

The Masks We Wear

The examples we have looked at have all been about the sharing of *words*. Sometimes, however, 'the pain speaks for itself'. It is seen in the eyes, the body language and the tensions of those who suffer, and, try as they might to contain it, their vulnerability is evident to those with eyes to see. It is to a deeper consideration of 'masks' and how we use them that we now turn.

The wearing of masks is for most (if not all) people, a fact of life. Consciously or not, we relate to others as we think we *should*: as the successful businessman who has everything and everyone at his fingertips; as the capable career-woman holding down a full-time job, with a spotless household and ever-attentive to her children; as the patient carer who never tires of serving the needs of her elderly relative. We behave as we think we should, and only in the privacy of our own 'space' do we ease off the image, look in the mirror, and see the reflection – often strained, tired and surprisingly ordinary.

The wearing of masks is not a new phenomenon nor is it necessarily a negative one, but it is a particularly post-modern one.[3] Whether we recognise it or not, masks play an important part in contemporary culture. For example, the post-modern understanding of the self has been described in terms of being a 'powerless victim' or 'vulnerable self'. What does this mean? Clearly, it is impossible here to do anything more than sketch what we mean, but is important to do so because it helps us to understand how significant and difficult any choosing to remove a mask may be, and, equally, how pertinent it may be to speak of some masks, at least, in positive terms.

In summary, then, the post-modern self is characterised by a loss of confidence and loss of trust, not only in other people, but in formerly accepted frameworks of reality and rationality. He is no longer sure of his identity. In his isolation, disorientation and insecurity, reality becomes what he creates it to be (a personal construct) and he lives with the constant threat of violence and conflict from 'them' – whoever 'they' may be. He reacts to and copes with this threat and his loss of identity by taking on and discarding a pastiche-personality of masks and images. He chooses to be who he wants to be. Intimacy with others becomes too demanding, nobody takes anybody (including themselves) seriously, and the self is overwhelmed by an inner sense of imprisonment and powerlessness. Indeed, within the post-modern framework, the whole idea of 'community' becomes anathema!

Nevertheless, people do live within communities, and they do – however tentatively – relate to one another within them. Masks are, indeed, worn, and knowing how to 'manage' them becomes all the more important. Our emphasis, so far, has tended to be towards the virtue of *removing* the mask, risking disclosure and choosing to be vulnerable. There is, however, another possibility.

When a clown enters the circus ring, he lays aside his daily life in order to give fun to others. Whatever he is going through – good and bad – he puts on the face paint, dons the enormous shoes and baggy trousers and goes out to make people laugh. There are two movements: a *laying aside* and a *putting on* of the mask – for the sake of those around him. There is a sense in which the kenosis, the 'self-emptying' of the Son of God, of which we spoke in Chapter 2, reflects those same two movements. He 'emptied himself', laid himself aside, and put on the 'mask', taking the form of a slave and 'being born in human likeness' (Phil. 2:7). Thus he 'contains' or limits himself in order to free himself to serve the Father and humanity.

Masks, then, can be positive gifts *for the sake of the other*. For the clown, the mask is not a denial of the clown's personality, but the means by which a part of that personality is revealed and focused. A mask both conceals *and* reveals. In the same way, Jesus put on, as it were, the mask of a slave in order to reveal the reality of his servanthood. What saves a clown from being a hypocrite (in the negative sense), what saves Jesus from being a divine being in a human shell, is that the mask is not a pretence but part of the reality. The human face of God in Christ is not God pretending to be human. It is a revelation of the glory of God which embraces humanity.

It would be easy to think of vulnerability in the context of community solely in terms of laying aside the mask. It is not as simple as that. Putting on a mask, revealing only as much of ourselves as necessary, is often the only way we can be fully available to serve others. They do not always need to know our angst and our fears, nor even our deepest joy. What matters is that we are aware that we are doing it and not fooling ourselves. What matters is that there are people with whom we can 'be real', who love us through and beyond the masks we wear. What matters is that we lay aside our masks when we come before God in prayer.

There is a cost to wearing a mask. That too is part of the cost of vulnerability. At such times, we need to respect each other's masks, charging neither ourselves nor others with hypocrisy, when what is, in fact, necessary is space for the Spirit to do her work of cleansing and purifying within the enclosure of our own hearts. Those who are leaders in the Christian community know the cost and the necessity of wearing masks. They know too the freedom and release of sometimes allowing them to be laid aside.

> *When a man becomes a clown he makes a free gift of himself to the audience. To endow them with the saving grace of laughter, he submits to be mocked, drenched, clouted, crossed in love. Your Son made the same submission when he was crowned as a mock king and the troops spat wine and water in his face . . . My hope is that when he comes again, he will still be human enough to shed a clown's gentle tears over the broken toys that once were women and children.*[4]

NOTES

1. cf. J. Zizioulas, *Being as Communion* (London, DLT, 1985). Also 'On Being a Person. Towards an Ontology of Personhood' in C. Schwöbel and C. Gunton (eds), *Persons, Divine and Human* (Edinburgh, T & T Clark, 1992), pp. 33–46). The Cappadocian Fathers (late 4th century) understood God as Father, Son and Spirit existing *only* in relation the one to the others; their insights have been revitalized through the work of such theologians as Zizioulas, Pannenberg, Gunton and A. J. Torrance, amongst others, over the last fifteen years.

2. Henri Nouwen, *In the Name of Jesus: Reflections on Christian Leadership* (London, DLT, 1989), pp. 10–11, 31 and 50–1.

3. When the Greeks wore masks in their tragic plays, the mask was 'neutral': it simply allowed them to be whichever character was appropriate. It was only later that their word for 'mask' – υποκριτης (hypokrites) – came to be understood in a negative way. For a fuller exploration of the post-modern understanding of masks, see, for example, J. R. Middleton and B. J. Walsh, *Truth is Stranger than it used to be: Biblical Faith in a Postmodern Age* (London, SPCK, 1995).

4. Morris West, *The Clowns of God* (London, Hodder & Stoughton, 1981).

5

Living Vulnerability: Leadership

The lecturer had been warm in his approach. He had spoken of the need to be open with others, to allow them to tell their story and not be judgemental in one's reaction. The person listening sensed empathy and warmth. He had held within himself, for the whole of his adult life, a sense of guilt and shame. Perhaps this person, a trusted member of staff, would be someone who would understand.

A few days later, when they were having coffee together, the student took the opportunity to reflect on the lecture. As he built up courage he began to speak his truth. As he touched his reality he saw the shock in the tutor's face. The lecture had been good but the lecturer could not handle the student's truth. The student was left vulnerable in an inappropriate way.

Whenever we are in a position of responsibility towards others we are open to our own and others' expectations of the 'leader'. In the example above, it may well be that the tutor and the student have very different perceptions of the tutor's role. Indeed much of the vulnerability of leadership will be the tensions caused by the clash of expectations.

Different styles of leadership will also create their own areas of vulnerability for those being led. In the exchange of power which takes place in any relationship there is the potential for healing or for destructive forces to be at play. Awareness of the ways in which we exercise authority is crucial. In reflecting on authority and power we learn as much from the times when we have got it wrong as when we can feel that we were nearer the mark. That too is the way of vulnerability.

In this chapter reflection on Jesus as a 'leader' and the exploration, albeit brief, of the biblical background to 'authority' and 'power', together with reflection on pastoral experience, lead us to offer a model of leadership. Against the ultimate need to surrender all to God, the need for particularity and discernment in the exercise of authority is advocated.

Jesus the Vulnerable Leader

This exercise of authority together with a discerned use or relinquishment of power is Jesus' chosen way of leadership. He does not deny his authority. From the manifesto of Luke 4 to the commission of Matthew 28, from the casting out of devils to the commission to forgive sins (John 20), Jesus acknowledges that he has a God-given authority which he exercises. What makes his leadership vulnerable is the power by which he exercises that authority. It is the power which points away from himself and towards the Father. It is the power which leaves people free to make choices. It is the power which attracts people by its integrity and love rather than by its force. It is a power which dares to become vulnerable to the loving attention of a woman with a jar of nard and copious tears, and silently vulnerable to those who would kill him. As Jesus exercises his authority it is clear that his power is expressed in ways which best help those to whom he ministers. There is always particularity and discernment. Whilst he accepts the ointment of the woman, he lets the rich young man, equally loved, walk away from the challenge. It is this particularity and discernment, this transparency to God combined with vulnerability to humanity which incarnates the divine ministry and which may inform ours.

Authority and Power

To establish any meaningful definition of 'authority' and 'power' is difficult, for the nature of both is complex and overlapping. Often we are left using pairs of words or phrases: authoritarian and authoritative,[1] extrinsic and intrinsic authority,[2] 'authority from above' and 'authority from below',[3] and conferred or natural authority. The danger is that we contrast types of authority rather than recognising the reality that any leader uses many different types of authority. To become aware of this reality is to become more discerning about ourselves and others. By our awareness and discernment, led by the Spirit, we may better conform our use of power with that of Christ.

In the New Testament, 'authority' is usually the translation of the Greek εζουσια, 'exousia', which strictly means derived or conferred authority,[4] with the recognition that all authority derives ultimately from God. The word 'power' too may be a translation of the same word or may translate the greek δυναμις, 'dunamis', which generally indicates ability, abundance, power, might, and even violence.[5] In Hebrew Rabbinical literature the Hebrew equivalent of 'dunamis' is a quality of God, literally 'the Power', a usage reflected in the New Testament when Jesus speaks in Matthew 26:24 of sitting at the right hand of Power. For biblical Greek, the word 'power' captures for us that personal power of the living God revealed in Jesus through the Holy Spirit.

It is clear that for the Christian leader the relationship with God is central to the faithful exercise of power of any kind and that such power is in all circumstances accountable to God. Somehow we need a model of authority which recognises that while we operate as those who are open to the Holy Spirit, we are also tempted and sometimes not without sin – a model which recognises the reality that

Whatever the strength of our love, and however Spirit-inspired we may be, our motives are always mixed and impure, and we are always susceptible to sin. Only the Son of God was motivated by pure love and service of his Father and of humanity.[6]

We need a model which 'connects' the power of the Most High and our knowledge of our frailty as we seek to be close to Jesus, a model which is applicable to the Christian doctor or social worker as well as to a bishop or a nun, a model which reflects both the appropriate use of power and of powerlessness.

Conferred and Derived Authority[7]

A working model might recognise that any leader has a combination of the authority invested in them by nature of the position they hold ('conferred authority') and another authority which derives from personal, situational and relational factors ('derived authority'). These two kinds of authority are the two ends of a continuum. Most often we work somewhere in the middle of the range, but there are times when it is appropriate, under God, to work at the limits, to take risks.

Conferred authority may be defined as that authority which is conferred on us by nature of our commissioning, appointment, the authority which we have by nature of our rank, title or status and the authority we have invested in us as those who receive the tradition and the necessary training. There is a conferred authority we receive from God, not least by nature of our Baptism into 'the person of Christ' (Jerome's translation of 2 Corinthians 2:10) by the power of the Holy Spirit. There is also an authority which is conferred upon us, rightly or wrongly, by others who – by their consent to their perceptions of our authority – give it credence. In fact, without this consent our conferred authority is largely in vain. St John Chrysostom makes the point well:

Shepherds have full power to compel the sheep to accept the treatment if they do not submit of their own accord. It is easy to bind them when it is necessary to use cautery or the knife, and to keep them shut up for a long time when that is the right thing, and to introduce different kinds of food one after another, and to keep them away from water . . . You cannot treat men with the same authority with which the shepherd treats a sheep . . . the decision to *receive* treatment does not lie with the man who administers the medicine but actually with the patient. [our italics][8]

Derived authority is that authority which is, in part, a reflection of our character: the authority that comes from our ability to make meaningful relationships, the authority we have as a result of our natural abilities and charms, the authority we have as a result of our capacity to reflect on our life experience and our work and to learn from that reflection. For Jesus and for us, perhaps the most potent kind of derived authority is that which stems from a life lived in relationship with the Father through the power of the Holy Spirit, that is, a life which is its own prayer, a life of integrity, a life where what we 'say with our lips we believe in our hearts and what we believe with our hearts we show forth in our lives'.[9] Such a life is lived not according to 'ought' and 'should' nor according to the conventions of society but rather in response to the inner voice of love, the Spirit's breath. There may be other areas of 'derived authority' too – in particular the authority which we or others, often subconsciously, transfer from another area of expertise, for instance, by assuming that a teacher can necessarily teach the faith or that a GP or MP makes a good member of General Synod because they have authority/status in another area of life. There is also the authority, the power we exercise over other people, by being ourselves people with needs whether they be real or imagined, known or unknown, per-ceived by us or by others.

It is, perhaps, when we have conferred authority which is matched by the derived authority of a life of integrity that we discover the great Christian leaders. They are not necessarily perfect. Perfection is not the point, but they are whole, wholly given to God, transparent in love, allowing all that they are to be surrendered to his will and submitting all their authority to his authority, love and power. By their fruits you shall know them (Matt. 7:6).

Whatever way we exercise authority there are risks and vulner-abilities which may or may not be appropriate. If we are working towards the 'conferred authority' end of the scale, we are at risk of exercising power outside of any context of relationship, trusting only in our status and in our own judgement. It is potentially the most abusive of authorities for when it is exercised without regard to God or others, and is motivated by self-interest, it can lead to the worst atrocities that the world has known. It can so easily be a 'cold-blooded' use of power – a power which dehumanises all involved. It is most dangerous when its use is matched by blind obedience. Part of the risk at this end of the scale happens when we have ceased to listen to those we trust to reflect honestly to us our understanding of where God is leading. Instead we have built our Kingdom within and called it God's. The authority that perverts conferred authority into running one's own kingdom is not an option for those who follow Christ. The 'power' needs always to be 'contained' so that it is exercised in surrender to the Father and in an appropriate way for the sake of those we serve. As we have argued in Chapter 4, it is highly significant that when Jesus is at key moments of his ministry his dependence on the Father, through the Spirit, and his need for a small group of friends is highlighted. Exercising such power, in a life surrendered to the Father, may mean taking a stand and suffering for it. It may even mean dying. Those who exercise such power will not seek their own glory.

Luke's Jesus is both a dramatically powerful figure and one who shares the fate of all God's prophets (4:24). The nature and scope of Jesus' present exercise of power is strictly limited. He does not come forward as a potential power figure in the structures of this world using miraculous powers to establish his position (4:23; 9:51–6). He can be and is rejected, and by God's will he ultimately submits to destruction by his enemies.[10]

Authority exercised at the conferred end of the scale, without real and sometimes critical feedback from those we serve, may make us vulnerable to false praise or blame. Those who give consent to our authority may be consenting to an authority we do not rightly have. They may imagine us to have some secret knowledge, some sanctity which by osmosis will transfer to them. There are always those who want Jesus' power without themselves becoming vulnerable. We cannot collude with them by allowing them to seek that power through their misunderstanding of the nature of our authority. Nor can we collude with those who criticise and judge us because they are running away from their own response to the Christ to whom we witness. Nor can we collude with ourselves in ever thinking we have got it right and others are wrong. Whether we are praised or blamed, it is seldom helpful to jump to an immediate response, to inflate our ego or to justify ourselves. It is better that we listen carefully and allow what we hear to be carried into prayer, into supervision and/or Spiritual Direction so that we may discern where reality lies. It is a costly way of ministering but one which takes full account of our frailty and the frailty of others.

At the other end of the scale is where the authority appears to be purely 'derived'. Here too there is the danger of inappropriate vulnerability. To depend on natural authority can, all too easily, be to depend on natural charm. It can very easily be an area where people are manipulated, consciously or subconsciously – a manipulation which may be effected either by the leader or by those in their care. Authority and power are always open to deception and self-deception, and our ability to rationalise our needs in terms of ministry to other people hardly needs spelling out. Even powerlessness can have its own power and can be highly intoxicating. To be powerless is to be victim. To be powerless in following the way of Christ, in surrender to the Father, is to recognise that power lies not in our being a victim but in the surrender.[11] We cannot afford to sanctify 'powerlessness' in itself. It is only redemptive when it is surrendered to God. Surrendered to God, the invitation may be not to submit but to struggle for justice. Both 'power' and 'powerlessness' can become idols with inherent and deep dangers.

For all its dangers, this end of the scale can also be the place where we drop all masks and allow our humanity to exercise its authority in helping others. It can be the area where we are most receptive to God's power, most aware of our own powerlessness.

> *A visit to a hospital consultant may be brief and can only be possible because the patient recognises and trusts the consultant's conferred authority to know the facts of the case, and trusts that consultant to have knowledge which will be of benefit. Over a period, the relationship may well become more balanced as the consultant gets to know the patient and as they together face the reality, say, of a terminal illness. Indeed, at the death bed, the consultant, who was first seen as the bearer of healing powers (their conferred authority, primarily but not exclusively), may be able to offer little but their warm humanity (clearly working now at times more from the 'derived authority' end of the spectrum). To allow that relationship to develop and grow, to let the patient become the one who helps the consultant face death, will involve many layers of vulnerability and openness on both people's part. In negotiating those layers and allowing the relationship to change, there will be different power exchanges.*

The consultant, once dressed in the white coat, with a dangling stethoscope and multitude of pens that hid her nakedness, may need to let go of status, and the patient who came to the clinic for the first time with few obvious therapeutic skills and a great need may be clothed, on the death bed, by gifts of healing which touch, among others, the consultant. The patient may reveal a clarity of perception and serenity of acceptance by which is witnessed a depth of derived authority. By such transactions of power, powerlessness and authority, many are blessed.[12]

In working in this area, where our conferred skills and knowledge give way to simple humanity, we need to be aware of the risks but not overcome by them. Love is born of taking risks, not playing safe.[13]

There are, of course, risks right across the scale, risks that emphasise the need to keep our relationship with God strong in order that we might be supported and discerning, risks which remind us of the need to 'contain' our use of power to suit particular circumstances, and, because we are human and liable to make mistakes, risks that remind us of the need to check things out, to be accountable to others who reveal a life of Christian integrity.[14] Commenting astutely on the healing of the woman with the haemorrhage of blood, Nolland suggests:

[The woman] needs to see that it is contact with Jesus himself that she needs and not simply anonymous access to his power. Power in religion without personal relationship and public commitment is little better than superstition or magic.[15]

Discernment and Particularity

Mostly we live not at one or other end of the scale but with combinations of conferred and derived authority, discerning through prayer, listening and openness to God, how best we might serve others. Maybe a simple example can make this clear.

A lady went to church, full of guilt, knowing that she needed

> *forgiveness. The priest, aware of his own frailty and, less con-*
> *sciously, of his desire to 'belong', wanted to be alongside the*
> *congregation and so when it came to the absolution said 'we' and*
> *'our' rather than 'you' and 'your'. It was understandable, but the*
> *woman needed to hear someone say, as Jesus said to the woman*
> *in Luke 7:48, 'Your sins are forgiven.'*

There may be all sorts of ways one could argue this example, but it shows clearly that discernment is needed about how we serve others – sometimes by becoming 'powerful' rather than powerless, by speaking solely from our conferred authority when our derived authority feels to be only weakness.

To return to the incident at the beginning of the chapter, we may see again how conferred authority and derived authority have been confused. It is all too easy to hand ourselves over to 'experts' and then stop discerning what is happening, thinking that 'they' must know the answers. In matters affecting the Spirit we do well to recognise that not everyone who has 'conferred authority' has the life experience or the ability to listen that comes from the 'derived authority' end of the spectrum. The student had recognised the undoubted conferred authority of the tutor. What he had not discerned was the derived authority. Did his life, rather than his words, indicate that he might be able to listen at depth; was he worthy of trust? In submitting to authority, as well as in exercising it, we need to 'test the Spirits'.[16] Often, in making ourselves vulnerable to others, it is the discernment of another's 'derived authority' which may indicate that we are safe to divulge personal information, whatever 'conferred authority' that person may also exercise. It is our life in Christ which will be affirmed or confused by those to whom we give most trust.

The 'Kenosis' of Authority

What this means in practice is that we hand over the way in which we exercise authority to God and to the needs of the people we serve. There is both surrender and submission. It is by our surrender to God that our submission to human authority and our exercise of human authority is directed. In Jesus' own ministry we may see this in practice in three incidents. There is the incident, when Jesus is twelve, when he both acknowledges the primacy of his relationship to the Father but also, within that, total surrender; 'he went down with them and came to Nazareth and was obedient to them' (Luke 2:51). There was also the time when Jesus came to be baptised by John, and John hesitates. Jesus contains his power, using it only to encourage John, and so Jesus is baptised. It is in his submission to Mary and Joseph and to John the Baptist that Jesus shows his 'handing over' of power, the ministry of 'passive activity' (see Chapter 7) which culminates in the Cross. There is also the incident of the foot washing in John 13, where Jesus is stripped and appears powerless in his servanthood but insists on washing Peter's feet. Always there is particularity and discernment. The kenosis is not about eschewing power. It is rather about using the appropriate power to serve God's purposes in those for whom we care. It is ultimately about surrender.

What is paramount is our surrender to God and our willingness not to seek for black-and-white solutions but to discern the will of God in every situation. There will be times when submission is right and others when it is not, times when we should speak out, times when we should necessarily stay silent. To live with this level of discernment is to choose the way of vulnerability, to live with risk and to sometimes suffer wounding as a result. As leaders, the power we have is not the raw human power which seeks only itself. It is rather the power which comes from God, God's 'dunamis', that dynamic power which does not flow from us but through us, as we are surrendered to his will. Perhaps nowhere is this made more clear than when Jesus commissions his disciples to bear fruit in his name. The word Jesus uses to appoint his disciples is the same word, τιθεναι ('tithenai'), that he uses to speak of laying down his own life. It is a word which implies laying down horizontally, surrendering oneself. Jesus lays down his life for his friends. He expects his friends to lay down their lives for each other and for God. This is the nature of leadership, a leadership one accepts because of a sense of trust and confidence in God. It is an acceptance of the power of God. Anthony Bloom puts it this way:

Surrender means such an act of trust and confidence that you can put yourself unreservedly, joyfully, by an act of freedom, into the hand of God, whatever, because you are sure of him, more than you are sure of anything else . . . these are the words of Jesus, 'No one is taking my life from me, I give it freely.' This is surrender.[17]

NOTES

1. Ian T. Ramsey, 'On not being judgemental', *Contact* no 30, March 1970.
2. Richard Holloway, *Dancing on the Edge* (London, Fount Paperbacks, 1997).
3. Jean Vanier, *The Scandal of Service* (London, DLT, 1997), p. 45.
4. J. Y. Campbell in Alan Richardson (ed.), 'Authority' in *A Theological Wordbook of the Bible* (London, SCM, 1957).
5. See Nigel Turner, *Christian Words* (Edinburgh, T & T Clark, 1980), p. 333.
6. See Chapter 2.
7. This model makes no great claims. It has come about as a result of reflection on twenty years of ministry, twenty years of falling and being helped up again, and a life of trying to follow Christ. Nothing more.
8. St John Chrysostom, *6 Books on the Priesthood* (London, SPCK, 1964), p. 56.
9. A childhood prayer used by members of the RSCM.
10. J. Nolland, *Luke*, 3 vols (Dallas, Texas, Word, 1989), p. 206.
11. John's gospel reveals this attitude as Christ lives his passion – a monarch reigning from the tree.
12. This image is a reflection of my own experience of my wife dying of Motor Neurone Disease – an image brought into focus by Sheila Cassidy, in *Sharing the Darkness* (London, DLT, 1988), pp. 61–4.
13. cf. A. V. Campbell, *Moderated Love: A Theology of Pastoral Care* (London, SPCK, 1984), p. 28. 'Patients, as much as doctors, struggle against such a revaluation of medicine, since it leaves them where they truly are, still vulnerable, still mortal. Yet there is a more solid kind of hope in such a relationship than that which medical idolatry offers.'
14. Such people may be part of the hierarchy or may be not.
15. Nolland, p. 423.
16. 1 John 4: In 'testing the spirits', we are not judging the people who influence us. We are seeing whether the influence is drawing us to God or away from him.
17. Anthony Bloom in Norman Autton (ed.), *From Fear to Faith* (London, SPCK, 1971), p. 26.

6

Living Vulnerability: Humility

The newly ordained deacon was not sure what to expect as he called at the house. A short phone call from a friend of a young mother had only said that her child was ill and she needed someone from the church to come and talk. As he went in, he saw the four-year-old girl at play. She had a lump on her forehead, a tumour. Stripped so soon of the title and degree that had lengthened his name both ends, he was soon on the floor playing with balloons. Later, when the girl became worse, he would be stripped further. All he would do was hold her in the hospital ward when her mother could not be there. At the funeral he was stripped even more. There was nothing left and words could not fill up the gap. His arms, like the mother's, were empty. All he could do was commend the girl into God's hands and arms. Theology was in the being there, present and attentive, in the humility of being prepared to stay with others in their pain and in the bearing of pain which must be contained in order to serve others and in order to reveal love.

It is perhaps appropriate that one who is a deacon should face this situation, for a deacon is by definition a servant and a deacon, in serving Christ, learns very quickly that serving other people is very much the way in which that service is made real. Jesus himself speaks of himself as being 'among you as one who serves' (διακονια, 'diakonia', Luke 22:27) and in the passage from Philippians 2 Jesus is seen as the one who takes the form of a slave δουλος, 'doulos'.

We are left in little doubt that the way of Christ is the way of humble service and that a ministry which embraces vulnerability will be founded on humility. In this chapter we explore what humility means and how it affects our relationship with God, with ourselves, and with those we serve.[1] We see in the person of Christ that humility is the outcome of a relationship with the Father based on love and trust, and we explore how in pastoral ministry such a relationship enables our own laying aside of our garments and the putting on of the towel (John 13) as we follow Jesus in humble service.

Encountering God

In Philippians 2 we are encouraged 'in humility, to regard others as better than yourselves' (Phil. 2:3) and reminded that Jesus 'humbled himself' (2:8). In both cases the word used stems from one which, outside the Christian context, implied weakness, submissiveness, lowliness. In the Christian setting, however, the humility expressed in Philippians and elsewhere is raised from something puny to perhaps the highest Christian virtue. Jesus himself was humble (Matt. 11:29; 2 Cor. 10:1) and it is a virtue much to be admired (Matt. 18:4; 23:12; Luke 14:11; 18:14; Eph. 4:2; Phil. 2:3; Col. 3:12; 1 Pet. 5:5; Jas. 4:10). Indeed, God comforts the lowly (2 Cor. 7:6) and, more specifically, 'he lifted up the lowly' in being born to Mary (Luke 1:52). In that 'being born' the kenosis of Christ finds practical expression when God approaches a humble woman who consents to be the place of encounter where God humbles himself. In that conception, pregnancy and birth there is a many-layered encounter of Creator with creature.

> Where each asks from each
> What each most wants to give
> And each awakes in each
> what else would never be[2]

In his Spiritual Exercises, St Ignatius has the phrase 'permit the Creator to deal directly with the creature and the creature directly with his Creator and Lord'.[3] It is in this encounter between the person who recognises himself as a creature of the divine Creator and the God who created him that true humility may be discovered. For our part, it is the humility of the person who accepts their vocation to be the unique person that God has made. Humility then is not about meek submissiveness but rather about commitment to the life-long process of knowing and accepting our true selves and, in the process, of becoming as well as in the being, consenting to be available to God. It is, in the words of Phil. 2:8, about being 'obedient to the point of death' to this calling to the fullness of our humanity. This is the humility of Christ who, 'humbled himself, but did not do so by ceasing to be who He is. He went into a strange land, but even there, especially there, He never became a stranger to himself.'4

Humility of this kind cannot be isolated from the encounter with God which is all-pervasive. Catherine Lucas, a confirmed atheist and scornful of belief and believers, writes of her coming to faith in God as a time of recognition that God is in all things. She writes:

The understanding of God is a sense of coming home in the fullest sense, of finally knowing one's true nature, because everything we experience, from joy, love and acts of genius to pain, grief and destruction – all come from this source. And knowing that has taught me to be grateful for each breath . . . believing in God has nothing to do with arrogance. Instead it creates true humility, because it reminds us that everything we are is thanks to God, that we are each a speck in the divine whole.5

Encountering Ourselves

'Finally knowing one's true nature', as Catherine Lucas puts it, is, perhaps, the pinnacle of spiritual perfection. Certainly Jane de Chantal considers it so. She writes:

All God wants is our heart and He is more pleased when we value our uselessness and weakness out of love and reverence for His holy will, than when we do violence to ourselves and perform great works of penance. Now, you know that the peak of perfection lies in our wanting to be what God wishes us to be: so, having given you a delicate constitution He expects you to take care of it and not demand of it what He himself, in His gentleness, does not ask for.6

In those few words, Jane de Chantal captures the spirit of humility – the reverence for God, the obedience to his will and the acceptance of our frailty. Humility which is not based on self-knowledge so easily slips into a dangerous submissiveness which may encourage low self-esteem and manipulation by others. It allows others to build false images of who we are and to harbour false expectations of what we can offer. Vulnerability cannot be built on such illusions. Somehow, with a gentle touch, we have to be true to our own limitations as well as to the needs of others. In other words, we have, like Christ, to choose to accept our finitude. In his book *Poverty of Spirit*, Johannes Metz writes of Jesus' time in the wilderness being tempted by Satan:

'You're hungry,' he tells Jesus. 'You need be hungry no longer. You can change all that with a miracle. You stand trembling on a pinnacle, overlooking a dark abyss. You need no longer put up with this frightening experience, this dangerous plight; you can command the angels to protect you from falling . . .' Satan's temptations call upon Jesus to remain strong like God, to stand within a protecting circle of angels, to hang on to his divinity (Phil. 2:6). He urges Jesus not to plunge into the loneliness and futility that is a real part of human existence.[7]

In living with ourselves and with other people it is all too easy to try to forget our finitude, to hang on to some illusive and false strength which we like to imagine will save us from the human condition. But it is to the fullness of the human condition that we are called with all its vulnerability, risks, temptations and fears as well as its joys and delights. So St Paul reminds us that Jesus was obedient even to death and *therefore* was highly exalted.

Encountering Each Other

Such humility reveals itself not only in the encounter between the individual and God, but in encounters with other people. This is, of course, the context of Philippians 2 where St Paul is encouraging the Philippians to model their corporate life on the way of Christ who emptied himself. Such emptying is only possible in the context of relationships and the relationships themselves will indicate not only the need to be emptied but the 'form' of that emptiness.

Reverence for God, obedience to his will and acceptance of human frailty are again helpful pointers to living humbly with our God as we encounter him in others. St Benedict in his rule reveals how these pointers may strengthen the life of the Christian community. He writes, 'The first step of humility, then, is that a man keeps the fear of God always before his eyes (Ps. 35:2) and never forgets it' and continues 'he must constantly remember everything God has commanded.'[8] Reverence for God and obedience to God and, therefore, to those to whom authority has been given, lies at the heart of humility. But such reverence and obedience are not isolated from the attitude which is to be held by all in common – that Christ is in the other and to be reverenced there. In daily life the monks are to live in *mutual* obedience, love and service. It was in this community of each serving the other that the cenobitic tradition saw the kenosis of Christ being worked out. In Chapter 71 of the Rule, St Benedict writes:

Obedience is a blessing to be shown by all, not only to the abbot, but also to one another as brothers since we know that it is by this way of obedience that we go to God.[9]

Here is the core of Christian community – each serving the other; the whole theocentric rather than egocentric.

This reverence, obedience and acknowledgement of frailty permeates the whole Rule. Allowance is made for those who are weaker than others, provision made for mistakes and for forgiveness. In encountering others, some of whom may share our beliefs and many of whom will not, the path of humility bids us, too, to show reverence to others, obedience to God and an honest appraisal of frailty – our own and that of others.

Encounter with Struggle

In quoting the account of Jesus in the desert above, we are reminded that to choose to be true to our unique vocation is no easy option. It will involve struggles at many different levels. Writing of the vocation to the Carthusian life, a monk writes: 'He alone remains . . . who has felt a call in the very centre of his soul which is more powerful than any of the contradictory forces within and without him.'[10]

The reality and power of these forces that we feel as we seek to articulate and live the unique truth that God has made us are unavoidable. What else is our cross than these things?

It is the struggle between creaturehood affirmed and creaturehood denied: the struggle between a creaturehood admitted in all its poverty and vulner-ability, and creaturehood artificially concealed or built on what does not belong to it; between creaturehood affirmed as essentially relational and depen-dent, and creaturehood maintained as autonomous and self-sufficient, between 'I will not serve' and 'I come among you as one who serves.'[11]

But we can experience this struggle so that, rather than being mortally wounding, the pain of the struggle may, instead, inflict the wounds of love, the means by which God shapes us and moulds us more and more in conformity with his Son. Nevertheless, the desire to run away from the pain of the struggle can feel overwhelming and may take many forms. It is all too easy for us to be crushed by circumstances or by other people, all too easy for us to look for false security in unquestioning submission to authority, or in our own exercise of authority. Instead we are called to be the place of contra-diction where transformation and healing can occur:

We have got to live now in and through the dying, in order that we may bear witness to the resurrection life . . . If we live in this glorious perspective, we do not have to wait for the fullness of life after death. Life in God is here and now, experienced first and foremost by experiencing death. Do not be afraid to die, do not be afraid when you are overwhelmed by the sense of your own weakness and sin and muck and desolation. Let everything that is in you, and everything that is thrown against you by the power of evil, be held in Christ's healing power. Do not absorb it or be overcome by it, but let it in you meet Christ's power to heal; let it in you meet this almighty power of God, so that in you the mess can be transformed, answered.[12]

To know our poverty, to be prepared to accept 'the contradictory forces within and without', is to make oneself truly vulnerable, and that is the choice we make. It is the underlying choice, a decision to be with Christ wherever he is. It cannot be overemphasised that the choice is not to be a pious victim, but simply to bear the cost of *who* Christ wants us to be and *where* (i.e. in what specific life circumstances) Christ wants us to be – whatever is for his praise and glory. It is the choice not to hold on to our wealth, status and security (material, spiritual or whatever) but to be prepared to let go of everything and follow. It is the choice to make 'gods' of nothing but God and always to be open-handed, ready to give or to receive in the mutual exchange of love which is the hallmark of the perichoretic relationship within the Holy Trinity and between the Trinity and ourselves.

To choose humility as our fundamental attitude to God also raises, sharply, the question of how appropriate it is to be vulnerable in different situations and with different types of people. We have already noted that Christ's vulnerability was possible in the context of his relationship with his Father and with his closest followers. So with us. We too need to find our affirmation primarily in our relationship with God, but also in the context of circles of intimacy.

Christian leaders need to have humility not only before God but with a circle of friends and advisers with whom they too can touch the reality of their lives. It is all too easy for unexpressed needs to reveal themselves in leadership by manipulation, rationalisations and the control of situations so that they meet our needs rather than the needs of the people we serve. Humility in leadership means not only listening to the community and its needs but also to ourselves and our needs. Often those in leadership roles find this difficult. Within small communities – villages and towns – it can be hard for the 'professional' Christian to find the anonymity that may be required for objective help and support to be given. It may happen then that issues are not faced, but provide a permanent and disabling backdrop to the ministry the leader seeks to provide. Humility challenges this isolationism and invites those in leadership to come to an acceptance of the common need to find places where confidences can be shared and respected, where vulnerability is not seen as weakness but the raw material of holiness, the stuff of eternity.

Through the experience of being alongside people in Spiritual Direction, it is clear that many people in leadership feel this need to have a support network, though it may be expressed in a number of ways. Whilst there is a human resistance to interference in ministry, there is for many also a great sense of being left too much alone, to sink or swim without adequate 'supervision' in the professional sense or personal support in the purely human sense. The nature of vulnerability is that those who minister need both. They need a supervisory figure: one who shares with them in listening to God's will and way, who encourages, challenges, sets free, someone who shares with them the 'cure of souls' in a practical and realistic sense. Equally they need someone outside the hierarchy who offers 'unconditional positive regard'[13] and who is there for them as the reality of ministry impinges on their own journey and being. It may well be that there are a number of people who perform this soul-friendship. Jim Cotter calls such people 'godfriends'. He writes:

We need companions on the journey, godfriends . . . who will keep us to a chosen narrow way of pilgrimage, who themselves are becoming friends of God. Such friendship is usually askew, in the sense that one is there for the other, but not the other way round. If some find they can reverse roles in a mutual giving and receiving, they will need a third person from time to time to make sure that the blind are not leading the blind in mutual cosiness. There is a tough streak to discernment, and it is not easy to keep the process of review clear and uncluttered.[14]

Both these roles – the professional and the personal – are necessary support for those who seek to follow the Christ who made godfriends of his disciples.

Encountering Frailty in Our Leadership

Those in leadership roles will know only too well the sense of unworthiness to be a leader when one's own frailty is so apparent. Again, St Benedict is aware and cautions the abbot 'to distrust his own frailty and remember not to crush the bruised reed'.[15] Later, in the same chapter, he says of the abbot that he must not be 'excitable, anxious, extreme, obstinate, jealous or over suspicious'. In other words, leaders need to be aware of their own frailty so that it is not damaging their relationships with others or their own inner calm and prayerfulness. In so saying, St Benedict bids us take seriously our own development and spiritual health, not for selfish gain but in order that we might better serve God and others. The humility we have described lies at the heart of a leader's willingness to seek the necessary help and support.

How can this be? The question is not original. It is the question of Mary as the news of Christ's birth is announced. How can this be that God can actually use our apparent weakness, our poverty, our emptiness, our state of contradictions? It can only be because God loves us. It can only be when we recognise that love, a love we can trust at depth even when the going is rough.

Christ's Encounter of Love

Even Jesus needed that love to be affirmed. It is no coincidence that before Jesus goes into the desert he is baptised, that before he sets his face towards Jerusalem he is transfigured. The preparation for ministry is the affirmation of love; the voice which says to Christ and to us 'You are my child, whom I love'.

It is in the context of this love and trust that Christ encounters individuals and groups, that he enters conflict and suffering, that he reaches resolution in Gethsemane and surrender on the Cross. It is there, the place of 'primal love', that he and we discover that love cannot be quenched even by death.

This 'primal love' is the love which existed before the foundation of the earth, the love out of which Adam was created from the dust of the earth, the love that took humus and made humanity, the love that invites us to humility, the love that took the dust of death and blew it aside to reveal resurrection life – the love that endures through eternity.

Perhaps real humility is simply trusting in that primal love when we cannot even experience it, when with Christ we hang on our cross.

O my God, I believe not only in your infinite goodness which embraces the whole world, but also in that particular and wholly personal goodness which embraces me poor creature that I am. And that is why Lord, even when I see nothing, when I feel nothing, and when I understand nothing, I believe that all I am, and all that comes to me is the work of your love. I put myself in your hands, do with me whatever you wish, leaving me only the consolation of obeying you. So far as you call us, give us the generosity to answer your call, through Jesus Christ our Lord. Amen.[16]

Pastoral Encounters

We remarked in Chapter 5 that 'Love is born of taking risks, not playing safe.' So the humility leads us to take risks with Christ, daring to love and be loved in our service of others. Michael Ramsey makes the need for those risks clear:

In your service of others you will feel, you will care, you will be hurt, you will have your heart broken. And it is doubtful if any of us can do anything at all until we have been very much hurt and until our hearts have been very much broken.[17]

In terms of our relationships with other people, our seeming emptiness may be a sign of our identification with Christ, an identification of love. In pastoral encounters we may often feel that we have nothing to offer. We come, not with our agenda and our largesse, but with an open and receptive heart and ear, ready to respond. We come, with Christ, to ask 'What do you want me to do for you?', not to tell the other what they need. To return to the deacon at the beginning of the chapter, he comes stripped in the reality of the situation. Unless he can reveal love, he may not have opportunity to be of use to the family. He cannot hide behind titles and degrees, he cannot hide behind a bush of fear. He may rather trust the love that lies at the heart of humanity and divinity. He may identify with Christ, call silently upon his grace, and respond lovingly and naturally to the unfolding situation. He will need to use all his ability, all his understanding, gained through experience and through training, prayer and reflection, to relate theology and practice. But he will also need to listen with all his being to the small girl and those around her, and in them and beyond them to God. It is with this level of humility that he will be enabled to serve them 'with the mind of Christ'. Indeed, it is often when everything fails, when we share the utter powerlessness of the truly poor, that we find ourselves closest to the mind of Christ in letting go of everything except God alone.

It is in this willingness to become nothing but love that the good news is conveyed, and this love is not a sentimental love which avoids pain or covers it up by superficiality. It is, rather, Christ's love which dares to embrace pain, to absorb it, and allow it to be healed by the holding. It is the love which embraces insights gained from experience, training and prayerful reflection, so to be as alert as possible to the needs of others and to a deeper understanding of them. It is the love which consents to place itself in humble service at God's disposal.

> *Benedict's magna carta of humility directs us to begin the spiritual life by knowing our place in the universe, our connectedness, our dependence on God for the little greatness we have. Anything else he says, is to find ourselves in the position of 'a weaned child on its mother's lap' cut off from nourishment, puny, helpless – however grandiose our images of ourselves – and left without the resources necessary to grow in the spirit of God. No infant child is independent of its mother, weaned or not. No spiritual maturity can be achieved independent of a sense of God's role in our development.*[18]

NOTES

1. Part of our exploration will be to reflect on St Benedict's Rule, and what Joan Chittister calls his 'magna carta of humility'. See Note 18.

2. Edwin Muir, 'The Annunciation' in *Collected Poems* (London, Faber & Faber, 1960), p. 117.

3. Louis J. Puhl sj, *The Spiritual Exercises of St Ignatius* (Chicago, Loyola University Press, 1951), [15].

4. Barth, as quoted in Chapter 2.

5. Catherine Lucas, 'How I found faith' (London, *The Times*, 24 December 1997), p. 12.

6. F. de Sales and J. de Chantal, *Letters of Spiritual Direction* (New York, Paulist Press, 1988), p. 194.

7. Johannnes B. Metz, *Poverty of Spirit* (New York, Paulist Press, n.d.), p. 16.

8. *RB1980 Rule of St Benedict in English* (Collegeville, Minnesota, The Liturgical Press, 1982), [7].

9. *RB1980 Rule of St Benedict in English*, [71].

10. A Carthusian, *The Wound of Love* (London, DLT, 1994).

11. William Broderick SJ, in *The Way Supplement*, no. 52 (London, The Way, 1985), p. 87.

12. Mother Mary Clare SLG, *Fairacres Chronicle*, Winter 1988 (Oxford, SLG Press, 1988), p. 13.

13. Carl Rogers.

14. Jim Cotter, A Paper on the Cairns Network.

15. *RB1980 Rule of St Benedict in English*, [64].

16. Pope Benedict XV, further source unknown.

17. Quoted in Simon Stephens, *Death Comes Home* (London, Mowbrays, 1972).

18. Joan Chittister, *The Rule of Benedict* (UK, St Pauls, 1992), p. 62.

7

Living Vulnerability: Waiting

When I consider how my light is spent,
E're half my days, in this dark world and wide,
And that one Talent which is death to hide,
Lodg'd with me useless, though my Soul more bent
To serve therewith my Maker, and present
My true account, lest He returning chide;
'Doth God exact day-labour, light deny'd?'
I fondly ask; But Patience, to prevent
That murmur, soon replies, 'God doth not need
Either man's work or his own gifts. Who best
Bear his mild yoke, they serve him best, his State
Is Kingly. Thousands at his bidding speed
And post o'er Land and Ocean without rest:
They also serve who only stand and wait.'[1]

To 'stand and wait' does not come easily to most people. Whether it is queuing in the supermarket, waiting for a train, or knowing that you are somewhere on a council housing or hospital 'waiting list', 'standing and waiting' is an experience which most people would prefer not to endure. In a world where time is of the essence, where 'now' is what matters, and where the future is uncertain, the desire for present satisfaction and instant results is almost overwhelming. We are cajoled into believing that waiting is a waste of time – unnecessary and even wrong – and that if we choose to wait, then we are either lazy or odd.[2] Against such a background, Milton's sonnet is surprisingly apposite. Though it may not be 'at *his* bidding', thousands do, indeed 'speed And post o'er Land and Ocean without rest'!

One of the reasons why waiting is so unpopular is that it makes us vulnerable. We live in an age of action, and to act is to imply a certain control over what happens. We do what we choose, when we choose.[3] To be denied that possibility, or to choose *not* to act in any given situation is – apparently, at least – not to be in control. It is to be in the hands of others. It is to be at their mercy.

We began to explore the vulnerability of waiting in Chapter 3. There we spoke of waiting before God in prayer and of the place of silence, surrender and a deep longing for God. Such a longing as expressed in Psalm 63 –

O God, you are my God, I seek you, my soul thirsts for you, my flesh faints for you, as in a dry and weary land where there is no water

– such a longing creates its own vulnerability as the soul waits for an intimacy which only God can satisfy. Here, we shall look at Jesus' experience of waiting, and in so doing, discover that he became not a *powerless victim*, but a *vulnerable enabler*. By reflecting on Jesus' and our own experiences of waiting – chosen and not chosen – we shall explore the idea of *passive activity*, made possible in and through our relationship with 'the waiting Father',[4] through the Son and in the Spirit.

The 'Waiting' Son

Jesus' own experience of waiting may be understood in two particular ways. Firstly, in terms of the passage of time; secondly, in terms of choosing not to take action, a 'holding back' of his own ability to act in order to give others space to take action against him. Our study of these two aspects of waiting may be focused in the biblical use of two particular Greek words: ωρα(hora), meaning 'the hour', and παραδιδωμι (paradidomi), meaning 'to hand over to another'.

The use of the word ωρα, 'hora', although it appears in the Synoptic Gospels (e.g. Matt. 26:18, 45; Mark 14:35; Luke 22:14, 53), is particularly developed in St John's Gospel. In the Synoptics it is used exclusively with reference to the passion of Jesus. In John it is sometimes used with the definite article ('*the* hour') or a possessive pronoun ('*my* hour' or '*his* hour'), and sometimes with the indefinite article '*an* hour').[5] The former refer to a particular and significant period in Jesus' life, namely that defined in John 13:1 – 'Now before the Festival of the Passover, Jesus knew that his hour had come to depart from this world and go to the Father' – a departure which would be accomplished in his passion, death, resurrection and ascension. Jesus' first statement that 'the hour has come' (John 12:23) is immediately after his triumphal entry into Jerusalem on Palm Sunday. The goal of 'the hour' is his glorification, as the crucified, risen and ascended Lord.

Prior to John 12:23, however, there are a number of references which indicate that there was a period of waiting for Jesus. For example, in John 7:30 and 8:20 we read that despite his 'provocative' words, no one arrested Jesus 'because his hour had not yet come'. Jesus knew what was likely to happen: the Sanhedrin had already decided to kill him (John 11:53) and he had already been anointed for burial (John 12:1–8), but he had to wait for the time to be right.[6] In his humanity, he feared what lay ahead, and yet his relationship with and perfect obedience to his Father made the waiting possible.

It is significant that one of the Markan references to 'the hour' (Mark 14:41) occurs in conjunction with the verb παραδιδωμι, 'para-didomi' (to hand over). Jesus had been praying in the Garden of Gethsemane and returns, for a third time, to his sleeping disciples and says to them, 'Are you still sleeping and taking your rest? Enough! The hour [*hora*] has come; the Son of Man is betrayed [*paradidotai*] into the hands of sinners.'[7] For Jesus, the 'hour' was the hour of being 'handed over' or betrayed. The waiting (in temporal terms) was over; the waiting (in terms of his passion) had begun.

The verb *paradidomi* meaning 'to give, hand over to another' is occasionally used in respect of a thing or a commodity (e.g. 'authority' in Luke 4:6) or in the sense of handing down a tradition (e.g. Luke 1:2 cf. Acts 6:14; 16:4). It is most commonly used, however, to indicate a *person* being handed over to another, and is used both *by* Jesus (e.g. Matt. 10:19; 24:10; Mark 13:11; Luke 12:58; 21:16) and *in respect of* Jesus (Matt. 26:15; Mark 14:10; Luke 22:4, 6; John 19:11). W. H. Vanstone, in Chapter 2 of his classic text *The Stature of Waiting*, presents a study of the roots of this particular Greek verb in the Gospels of Mark and John. He comments:

What happens in both Mark and John when Jesus is handed over is not that he passes from success to failure, from gain to loss or from pleasure to pain: it is that he passes from doing to receiving what others do, from working to waiting, from the role of subject to that of object and, in the proper sense of the phrase, from action to passion.[8]

Jesus becomes, by his own initiative, one who is *done to* and who exposes himself to risk. He allows himself to be vulnerable to what others will do to him, even though that may be infinitely costly, painful and destructive to himself. His 'waiting' is not simply an inability to do anything about the situation. Rather, it is a conscious act of obedience to the Father which both enables and allows others to do their worst to him. Rather than becoming a helpless victim, he is the vulnerable enabler. Rather than becoming the epitome of powerlessness, he demonstrates the power of his powerlessness.

Whereas much of Jesus' early ministry might be described as 'prophetic activity' – that is, that he brings in, in his person, the Kingdom in word and deed – gradually (and especially after his 'hour' had come), 'prophetic activity' is replaced by what we might describe as 'passive activity'. 'Doing' in the sense of 'bringing to bear upon another' is replaced by 'being done to', a willingness to be present with another in such a way as to free them to do what is necessary, even at the expense of his own life. In a sense, therefore, even Jesus' passivity is active. He made what happened possible. It was his choice. He could, at any stage, have withdrawn from the situation – as, indeed, he did when the hour had *not* yet come (cf. Luke 4:30) – and opted out of his Father's purposes. That he did not, but rather chose the way of obedience, making himself vulnerable to others, was because of his security in relationship, through the Holy Spirit, with his Father, and because of his great love for humanity.

Our Experience of Waiting

Our own experiences of waiting are many and various. Sometimes it is a case of waiting without knowing what one is waiting for. Time seems to pass without significance. Often the waiting is a waiting in darkness, an awareness of the apparent 'absence' of God; a sense of emptiness and pointlessness. For example, an elderly gentleman who had led a full and very active life became increasingly depressed as he had to adjust to others doing things for him – cleaning his room, preparing his meals, washing and dressing him, feeding him. As he became physically less able, he became more and more emotionally withdrawn, despite continuing to be sufficiently intellectually agile to complete the *Telegraph* crossword each day. To him his waiting seemed empty and pointless. By contrast, a woman suffering from a degenerative disease of the brain which had rendered her unable to speak and totally dependent upon others for her physical needs, seemed to radiate a contentment and joy – even through the pain of her impending separation, by death, from her family – which enabled the family themselves to wait with her and to see some purpose in her suffering. *Her* waiting was 'full'.

Sometimes our experience of waiting is 'temporal', in the sense of waiting for something which is to take place at a particular time, such as a time of celebration – an anniversary, or Christmas, or a particular time which we are not looking forward to such as an operation or a difficult appointment.

Sometimes our experiences involve us in making a choice *not* to act, such as choosing to forgo treatment for a terminal illness or staying silent in the face of criticism. One of the skills which those in the public eye quickly have to learn is when it is worthwhile responding to criticism. Politicians are experts at side-stepping criticism in order to avoid upset. Even at the local level, knowing, for example, whether to respond to a critical letter in the local press or whether to ignore it and let it pass is a skill which even church leaders have to develop. Yet *not* to respond to criticism can open one to even more. It is a risky path to tread.

Sometimes our experiences of waiting are a mixture of all three. Whatever they are, they can make us vulnerable.

Occasionally our choosing not to act affects not only ourselves but also others. A parent, for example, who decides that the time has come to stop nagging her reluctant teenage daughter to do her homework risks not only the daughter's well-being and reputation, but her own as well. Yet, as all parents know, to hold back and allow one's children to make mistakes and discover their true responsibilities is one of the painful tasks of parenthood.[9]

Sometimes there seems to be little or no choice about waiting. If we are waiting for the result of an examination whether medical or academic, we have to be patient until the 'publication' date; we are in the doctor's or examiner's hands. They have the skills and the authority to make the assessment and we have to wait until they let us know the outcome. There is nothing we can do to bring about a resolution sooner. Or it may be that decisions about our future, whether in respect of schools, employment, accommodation, or even (in some parts of the world) our marriage partners, will be made by others on our behalf. In such circumstances, to await the outcome is to be in a very vulnerable place.

These are all very specific, comparatively small-scale examples. Vanstone points out, however, that despite our abhorrence of it, 'waiting' (or, in his terminology, the 'status of patient') is a much more common experience than we would care to admit.[10] The unemployed, the retired and the elderly are all, to some degree, in the hands of others. They are no longer directly responsible for their own maintenance and well-being, and their activities tend to have to be fitted around those of the more active members of their communities. Yet Vanstone also points out that in our complex, technological society, we are *all* increasingly dependent on external factors: if there is a power cut, then there is little we can do about it other than to light a candle and wait. We are in the hands of those others who can restore electricity to the system and enable us again to work on our computers, mow our lawns, or watch TV.

With such a breadth of experience of waiting, it is, perhaps, surprising that we find it so hard to bear, particularly when we are waiting for things which we may not want to take place but which we know are for the best. It is at such times that prayer becomes particularly important,[11] for it is prayer which is supremely the place of learning *passive activity*. It is the place of exploring possibilities, of being receptive – not waiting for God to act, but waiting for his will to be revealed. Donald Coggan reflects on the Hebrew understanding of 'waiting on God':

for a Hebrew writer to 'wait on God' was not to lapse into a state of passivity. There was much more to it than that! To wait is to be *willing*. The word 'expectancy' which we have used implies some action on God's part; but it involves also a willingness, even a desire and longing, to respond when God reveals his will. To wait is not to lapse into inactivity. It is to be ready to engage in action when God shows that the time for action is ripe.[12]

By choosing to place ourselves at God's disposal, by 'handing ourselves over' to him, whatever the outcome, we experience, in prayer, the security of utter dependence on his love and grace. To discover such a dependence in prayer enables us to begin to risk such passive activity in daily living. For if our ultimate security is in our relationship with God, what does anything else matter?

To apply such an approach to those in leadership is not to encourage irresponsibility and unaccountability. Nevertheless, it can free the 'activist' leader from always having to act, and the vulnerable leader from always having to hide his weakness. It can also be a catalyst for the growth of those who are being led.

The willingness of a leader to hand over to a community a particular decision affecting the life of that community speaks of one who is willing not only to share the task of discernment with others but also to risk the outcomes of that decision, whilst remaining in leadership of the community. In Chapter 3 of Benedict's Rule,[13] the abbot is encouraged to listen to the advice of all and only then make a decision. It is a very clear method of proceeding, but in practical terms it can mean listening to a large number of people.[14]

For example, in one case all those who led youth groups in a church were brought together for a number of meetings. They consulted the children and young people, and questionnaires were sent out to parents and to the wider congregation. Once all the opinions were sought, the minister drew up a proposal which clearly related to all the comments made but was not constrained by them. In this way, a consensus was eventually reached and a lasting pattern for youth work and worship established. It took time, energy and much prayer. It also meant that the minister had to 'carry the can' and ensure that further time was not spent re-visiting old arguments once a decision was agreed by the Church Council.

An alternative and much quicker approach would have been for the minister to stay very much in control and decide the way ahead without consultation. There would have been no 'waiting' in either the temporal or passive sense. The path he chose, however, was the more risky one. Firstly, he had to let go of his own desires for the future of the youth work and worship and trust that by prayer and careful listening the will of God would emerge. Secondly, the consultation process itself made him vulnerable to the influences (and criticism) of everybody else involved. Thirdly, once the decision was made, the minister as well as everybody else had to abide by it and take responsibility for it – whether or not he entirely agreed with the outcome.

In this instance the role of the minister was not so much hierarchical as to be an *enabler* of the community to discern the will of God. In so doing, he let go of control and chose to exercise his leadership through the powerlessness of listening. Such an approach makes many people feel uncomfortable; there will be those who demand that a leader leads clearly and actively 'from the front'. To choose not to do so can make a leader vulnerable to accusations of incompetence or even laziness. It is, in a sense, to choose to become a *vulnerable enabler*, and to choose to follow a path of *passive activity*.

The Kenosis of Waiting

To learn to 'stand and wait' is probably one of the hardest tasks for those in leadership. It must never become an excuse for laziness or inactivity where action is needed. The role of the 'prophet' in leadership must never be forgotten. Nevertheless, if a leader is to follow the example of the self-emptying Christ, there will be occasions when, through prayer, he or she discerns that their role is to be the more passive one of choosing *not* to act or react but to let things take their course, not rushing into things but discerning the next step and waiting for *God's* moment before acting.

For example, one Sunday after the morning service a parishioner lodges a complaint about her home group leader, and demands that the minister 'does something about him'. Several others have complained about his manipulative, overpowering style of running the home group. The leader concerned is 'holding forth' nearby with another member of the congregation. The minister is tempted to speak to him straight away, but discerns that now is neither the time nor the place for a confrontation, however justified and necessary. He chooses, instead, to take the matter into prayer over the next few days, and arranges to see the offending home group leader privately, before the home group next meets.

Indeed, it is common for those in leadership (both ordained and lay) to be 'collared' after a service by other members of the Christian community. Rarely is such a time appropriate for such an encounter. True attentiveness, without the pressures of time and situation, normally requires a more appropriate time and place.

To choose not to act immediately but to risk waiting is to choose to follow the one who waited in prayer in the Garden of Gethsemane, and yet who – when his 'hour' *had* come – obeyed his Father's will nevertheless. For Jesus knew that his being 'handed over' was not simply a matter of his betrayal by Judas, but was part of the wider framework of his Father 'delivering him up' for the sake of humanity. It was part of the divine intention (Acts 2:23) and had been fully anticipated by Jesus himself (e.g. Luke 9:44; 22:21–2). Though in his humanity and anguish in the Garden he may have lost sight of it for an instant, Jesus placed his hope and trust in his heavenly Father and walked the way of vulnerability to the cross. He knew that the best was yet to come.

And going a little farther, he threw himself on the ground and prayed that, if it were possible, the hour might pass from him. He said, 'Abba, Father, for you all things are possible; remove this cup from me; yet not what I want, but what you want.' (Mark 14:35–6)

NOTES
1. John Milton, 'On His Blindness'.
2. cf. W. H. Vanstone, *The Stature of Waiting* (London, DLT, 1982), pp. 49–50.
   Whenever, through the necessity and experience of waiting, our dependence 'comes home to us', it seems improper and offensive and generates tension, anger and

resentment. *Then, very frequently, we speak of our frustration, and, in doing so, we disclose our assumption that the waiting 'role', the condition of dependence, the status of patient, is improper to us, a diminution of our true function or status in the world, an affront to our human dignity.*

3. According to Victor Frankl in *Man's Search for Meaning* (London, Hodder & Stoughton, 1964), 'Choice makes us human.' What matters is that in the final event we can choose what *meaning* we give to a situation of waiting.

4. Helmut Thielicke, *The Waiting Father: Sermons on the Parables of Jesus* (London, James Clarke & Co Ltd., 1959).

5. For further discussion of John's use of 'hora' meaning *'an hour'*, see R. E. Brown, *The Gospel According to John* (New York, Doubleday, 1966), Appendix 1(11) pp. 517–18.

6. It is important to distinguish between χρονος (chronos), a space or period of time, and καιρος (kairos), denoting more the content and significance of a particular moment in time. It is significant that in a number of instances (e.g. Matt. 26:18 cf. John 13:1) the synoptists use the term 'kairos' in an equivalent place to John's use of 'hora'. For Jesus' own use of 'kairos' in respect of himself and others, see John 7:6.

7. cf. Mark 13:11, where Jesus warns his followers of the trials and persecutions they must expect. In that verse, there is reference to them being 'handed over', and also the use of 'hora' in respect of their being given the right words to speak at that particular moment of crisis.

8. Vanstone, p. 31.

9. It is interesting, in this context, to reflect on the character of the father in the parable of the Prodigal Son in Luke 15. Helmut Thielicke in *The Waiting Father*, p. 21, observes: ' . . . wordless, the father watches the departing son . . . The father . . . will wait for him and never stop watching for him. Every step he takes will give him pain . . . But the voice of his father in his heart will follow him wherever he goes.'

10. Vanstone, Chapter 3.

11. cf. Ignatius of Loyola, who in his section of *The Spiritual Exercises* on 'Rules for the Discernment of Spirits' speaks of the need to learn patience in desolation:

One who is in desolation should strive to preserve himself or herself in patience. This is the counter-attack against the vexations which are being experienced. One should remember that after a while the consolation will return again . . .'

From Ignatius of Loyola, *The Spiritual Exercises and Selected Works*, ed. George E. Ganss SJ (New York, Paulist Press, 1991), p. 203.

12. Donald Coggan, *God of Hope* (London, Fount, 1991), pp. 30–1.

13. Justin McCann (tr.), *Rule of St Benedict* (London, Sheed & Ward Ltd, 1976).

14. There are echoes of this approach in much recent work in Community Development. See, for example, George Lovell, *Analysis and Design* (London, Burns & Oates, 1995).

8

Living Vulnerability:
Hope

All shall be well and all manner of thing shall be well[1]

Hope, for the Christian, is no false optimism. It is to live with the pain and vulnerability of the present in the constant awareness that all that was, is and shall be has – once and for all – been redeemed through the death and resurrection of the Son of God. It is to live in the continuum of the past, present and future *in the light of that future*, where what shall be shapes the meaning of all that is.

A Context of Hope

It is hope that makes waiting possible. Children will put up with sitting through a 'boring' concert if they know there will be a reward of a bag of chips at the end. A family will cope with the pressures of living in cramped accommodation if there is the promise of a spacious house around the corner. An elderly person will wait for an operation to remove a cataract in the hope that vision will be restored.

In Chapter 7 we emphasised again the importance of security of relationship with God, and prayer as the primary means of nurturing that relationship. The context for that relationship – both for the incarnate Son and for us – is the overarching purpose of God to restore all things to himself:

In the days of his flesh, Jesus offered up prayers and supplications with loud cries and tears, to the one who was able to save him from death, and he was heard because of his reverent submission. Although he was a Son, he learned obedience through what he suffered, and having been made perfect, he became the source of eternal salvation for all who obey him. (Heb. 5:7–9)

Jesus bore the pain of being human. He was able to accept the suffering of the cross because he trusted his Father and knew that his obedience to him, in this act of self-giving love, was part of the bigger scheme of things, a vital chapter in the bigger story of God's plan of salvation for the whole cosmos. The cross and resurrection pointed backwards, yes, to deal with all that had driven God and humanity apart, but it also pointed forwards, a sign of the redemption of all that continued and continues to separate human beings from God and from one another, and a sign also of the promise that God's Kingdom will come on earth as it is in heaven. Anthony Thiselton puts it this way:

Even the events of the ministry of Jesus point beyond themselves to the resurrection; and his resurrection and the event of Pentecost point, in turn, to yet future modes of promise and fulfilment.[2]

The saving work of Christ is set within a context of hope. If we return again to that classic passage about the self-emptying of the Son of God (Phil. 2:5–11), we are reminded that his self-emptying was not so much a 'loss' or 'veiling' of his divinity but rather an embracing, an acceptance of a vocation to obedient humiliation and death. His chosen vulnerability was a gift received from the Father, and offered for the sake of humanity. In the gospels, at those turning points of Jesus' ministry (especially in Gethsemane), we see something of the struggle which the human Jesus underwent in choosing to accept this gift of vulnerability. He was not a victim of imposed suffering over which he had no control; rather, his human will was moulded by the Holy Spirit, to the divine will, so that he could accept the gift of following the way of vulnerability. He went to his death willingly and obediently, trusting that God would vindicate him.

That vindication, and the glory which ensued, is evident in the second part of the passage from Philippians 2. From the depths of death and hell he was raised to life, and in his resurrection all of humanity's 'hell' was redeemed:

9. Therefore God also highly exalted him
   and gave him the name
   that is above every name,
10. so that at the name of Jesus
    every knee should bend,
    in heaven and on earth and under the earth,
11. and every tongue should confess
    that Jesus Christ is Lord,
    to the glory of God the Father.

Descent was followed by ascent; self-emptying by fulfilment; cross by resurrection and exaltation. Not that the human Jesus could *prove* that there was something better to come. There was, for him, no 'special guarantee' that his suffering and vulnerability would be worthwhile. If there were – if the human Jesus had particular, unique resources of strength and grace – then what good is his example to us when we face our own 'hell', our own places of vulnerability and suffering? No, his resource and his context were the same as ours: he lived in relationship with his Father through the Spirit, and he trusted in the Father's love. He placed his hope in him. For the vulnerable Jesus, and for us, there is a dimension of hope.

The Dimension of Hope

The dimension of hope has become especially important in Christian thinking and writing during the second half of the twentieth century. The collapse of modernity in the wake of two world wars, the holocaust, famine and environmental and ecological disaster, with its shattered illusions of humanity reaching ever-greater heights of achievement, progress and goodness, has brought about, for many people, an overwhelming pessimism about the future and a desire to live only for the present – for that is all there is to live for.

Into such a darkness comes the Christian dimension of hope. For the pain and vulnerability of past and present is held within the wider purposes of God. Just as

the pioneer and perfecter of our faith, who for the sake of the joy that was set before him endured the cross, disregarding the shame, [and] has taken his seat at the right hand of the throne of God (Heb. 12:2)

so may we who follow him along the way of vulnerability 'run with perseverance the race that is set before us' (Heb. 12:1b). The vulnerable woman, suffering from a degenerative brain disease (of whom we spoke in Chapter 7), was past running any races in the *literal* sense, and yet her focus was clearly on the promise of life in eternity with God. It was that focus, and the assurance and certain hope which it gave, which emanated in a quiet, joyful radiance to those around her. Indeed, it is this dimension of hope which makes it possible for any Christian, but especially those who lead, to accept a gift of vulnerability.

To think of vulnerability as a 'gift' may, at first, seem odd. Why should a God of love offer a gift which seems so costly to the one who receives it? The answer lies, surely, in the mystery of *all* gifts of grace – that is, that they are always given for the sake of the other (1 Cor. 12:7). In any relationship where Christian love motivates and the Holy Spirit directs, there is a gift of grace, and that grace is mediated through the listening, speaking and caring love of those within that relationship. For the ability to love and to be loved is always a gift of the One who *is* love. When a leader chooses to share her weakness, such grace is especially evident. Indeed, a gift of vulnerability, accepted and offered in the context of Christian love, can be a sign of hope and the means through which the Holy Spirit opens others out to a greater measure of God's love.

One of Jürgen Moltmann's (b. 1926) greatest contributions to theology has been his understanding of 'Christianity as eschatology' – of God's promise 'breaking in' from the future[3] – and his suggestion that the cross, resurrection and coming of the Spirit are not solely historical events of the past but also anticipatory events of the coming kingdom, when there will be no more pain (Rev. 21:4). It is tempting to think that to be vulnerable is, in some way, to deny that promise – even to deny the efficacy of the cross. In the midst of vulnerability and pain, it is easy to lose sight of the dimension of hope, either by denying the pain and so pretending to be *in*vulnerable or by becoming so immersed in it that there seems to be no future and no way out. Henri Nouwen describes it perfectly:

There is a deep hole in your being, like an abyss. You will never succeed in filling that hole, because your needs are inexhaustible. You have to work around it so that gradually, the abyss closes. Since the hole is so enormous and your anguish so deep, you will always be tempted to flee from it. There are two extremes to avoid: being completely absorbed in your pain and being distracted by so many things that you stay far away from the wound you want to heal.[4]

An admission of vulnerability within the dimension of Christian hope is an acknowledgement of the 'incompleteness' of that promised future. It is to acknowledge the continued existence of sin and present suffering and pain, but it is to do so *in the light of God's promises for the future.* Donald Coggan puts it in terms of being the 'interim people':[5]

We are the *interim* people, implicated in the griefs of this present world, as was our incarnate Lord, never pulling out from them, but always sharing in the groanings and yearnings of creation, and, at the same time, on the tiptoe of expectancy for the day when he shall reign.[6]

All through the centuries, Christians have lived with this tension, identifying with and bearing the pain of humanity, but trusting in God's promise of a kingdom fulfilled. From St Stephen onwards, the saint and martyrs of the Church have offered their own vulnerability – indeed, their very lives – as a sign of their trust and hope in God. Such a 'cloud of witnesses' (Heb. 12:1) stand as an encouragement to those who lead to accept a gift of vulnerability in the context of hope, and offer it back for the sake of those whom they serve.

When the son of an Anglican clergyman was knocked off his bicycle by a lorry, suffering head injuries which sent him into a deep coma, the clergyman and his family did not (indeed, *could not*) hide their anguish from their parishioners and friends. Their willingness to be vulnerable not only allowed those around them to express their own anguish at what had happened, but also freed them *all* to express their hope and trust in a God who heals. Each person – family, parishioners, friends – was able to stand alongside the other in their pain and darkness, not knowing what the outcome of their prayer and support would be, but trusting in the God of love nevertheless. For four days the child lay in a coma, all but dead. Some could find meaning in what had happened; others just needed someone to sit with them in the meaninglessness of it all. Yet through it all, there remained the underlying hope that God was still working in the emptiness and in the waiting. In an apparently hopeless situation, people's individual and corporate relationship with God, and their relationships with one another, gave them confidence to wait hopefully, and to keep praying for the child's healing. A week after the accident, he was allowed home from hospital with just a few cuts and bruises.

Hope and Vulnerability

When a woman spoke to a friend, for the first time, of the abuse she had received as a child, she did not know whether she would be listened to or rejected. Life seemed to be falling apart for her. She was at a point of desperation. To be rejected at *this* stage, too, would have been intolerable. What enabled her to take the risk of speaking was an underlying certainty that, even if her friend rejected her (as so many others had done in the past), God would not do so. Her friend supported and encouraged her: 'It will be okay,' he said. Although at the time she would not have been able to articulate it, she knew that her hope was in God and that she was therefore ultimately safe. In that sense, at least, her friend's words rang true.

It is not easy for those in leadership to risk the way of vulnerability. It takes a courage which is itself God-given. It is the dimension of hope, together with a recognition that to choose the way of vulnerability is itself a gift, which makes such risk-taking possible. As we have previously argued (see Chapter 4), discernment is vital: it may not always be appropriate for leaders to speak of their weaknesses. To do so in an inappropriate way is, in itself, a form of abuse. To do so outside of the dimensions of hope and gift of which we have spoken is to turn vulnerability into a self-indulgent form of idolatry – like a cross without resurrection (cf. John 5:6f). Yet for a leader to accept the gift and take the risk of offering it for the sake of those whom he serves is to become a sign of trust in the God of promise and the God of hope. For – just as Christ did to a thief on the cross at Calvary – a leader incarnates by *his* very presence, the presence of the God of hope, the God who (even on the cross) encompasses within himself, past, present and future.

Truly I tell you, today you will be with me in Paradise. (Luke 23:43)

NOTES

1. Julian of Norwich, *Revelations of Divine Love* (tr. Clifton Wolters), (Harmondsworth, Middlesex, Penguin, 1966).

2. A. Thiselton, *Interpreting God and the Postmodern Self: On Meaning, Manipulation and Promise* (Edinburgh, T & T Clark, 1995).

3. Moltmann's ground-breaking work, *Theology of Hope*, was published in 1964. Its impact on the theological world was enormous. It offered a theology based on the dialectic of the cross and resurrection of Jesus Christ, constructed in the light of God's promise for the future. Says Moltmann: 'From first to last and not merely in the epilogue, Christianity is eschatology, is hope, forward looking and forward moving, and therefore also revolutionising and transforming the present', p. 16.

The future is understood as ontologically prior to the present and the past, that is, the future draws the past and present towards it rather than emerging *out of* past and present. 'Promise' thus plays an important part in Moltmann's thinking. God 'breaks in', as it were, from the future. Creation itself is not static, but is understood as eschatologically orientated towards a redeemed messianic future – a new creation in the kingdom of glory – which has been opened up in Jesus Christ. (For more on Moltmann's *Theology of Hope*, see also R. Bauckham, *The Theology of Jürgen Moltmann* (Edinburgh, T & T Clark, 1995).)

4. Henri Nouwen, *The Inner Voice of Love* (London, DLT, 1997).

5. Donald Coggan, *The God of Hope* (London, Fount, 1991), p. 103.

6. cf. Rom. 8:18–25.

9

Living Vulnerability: Trust

I hear the Father's voice speaking to Jesus,
'Put out into deep waters'
and a virgin shall conceive
and bear a son . . . deep in the waters of her womb.
I hear the Father's voice speaking to Jesus
'Put out into deep waters'
and at the end of thirty years of hidden life
Jesus is baptised in the waters of the Jordan
and ministry begins
a ministry of teaching, healing, loving
but also conflict, misunderstanding, pain.
I hear the Father's voice speaking to Jesus
'Put out into deep waters'
as Jesus prays alone
the night before he dies
and so the awe-full cup is sipped
and through the deep waters of death
Jesus goes
and I, who claim to follow him
stand at the edge
wanting only to paddle
looking happily across the ocean
from this safe place.
But Jesus' voice is saying to me
Put out into the deep water
and come, follow me.[1]

The invitation to follow Christ is always an invitation to put out into deep water. Whatever our way of life, whether we are called to serve Christ in the mundane and ordinary or called to hold some authorised 'ministry' in the Church, we are called first and foremost to be 'in the person of Christ',[2] St Jerome's translation of 2 Corinthians 2:10. To be 'in the person', literally in the countenance, the presence, the face of Christ, means that the one mask we are to wear is *his* mask. People are to look at us and see Jesus; not an actor's mask of Jesus but the face that reveals Christ by its own love and pain transfigured and mingled into divine mercy and compassion. To be in his person means all that we can hope for, all that we can desire, has happened. We are embraced by the community of the Trinity, beloved, and blessed. To be 'in the person of Christ' also means that like him we will be wounded, that we will complete the Eucharistic action – not only taken and blessed but also broken and shared for the sake of the world.

We will have wounds, then, but maybe the choice is not so much about whether we are wounded. Many people are wounded by life. The question is perhaps more about what meaning we give to those wounds, and in the context of a chosen vulnerability, whether we will risk those further wounds which we will bear as a direct result of following Christ.[3]

In bringing this part of the book to a close, and before exploring, in the second part, what 'vulnerability' may mean for the life of the Church rather than for individuals, we need to reflect, once more, on aspects of our definition,[4] to see the risk and the attendant fears, to explore the way in which we may face those fears and turn from fear to love, from doubt and even from certainty, to loving trust.

Vulnerability as an Openness to Being Wounded

That God's people are wounded is not in question. The experience of life brings its own wounds, as does membership of any community. People are wounded even sometimes by the Church and its pastors. God longs, as ever, to reach out and bind those wounds. In Ezekiel 34 God reveals himself as the shepherd who will do that. In John 10 Jesus sees himself fulfilling that role but he does so by himself being wounded, by laying down his life for his sheep. It is by his surrender to the Father and his submission to what people will do to him, that is, by his consent to be handed over, that Christ actually brings healing. It is 'by his wounds that we are healed' (cf. Isa. 53:5). St John of the Cross captures the image in a shepherd boy who dies for love:

> After a long time he climbed a tree,
> and spread his shining arms,
> and hung by them and died,
> *his heart an open wound with love.*[5]

We, in the person of Christ, are wounded agents of healing. 'I feel called to the healing ministry,' said one lady, 'but I need healing so much myself, that I could not possibly put myself forward.' It is a natural reaction but it is based on a misunderstanding of the nature of power. It is the model that says that those who lead must know all the answers so that they can give from their bounty to those who know little. It is not the way with Christ who came not to exercise lordship but to reveal the power of servanthood, the power of surrendering woundedness to the Father. It is by his wounds that we are healed and it is by our wounds, offered to his service, that others may find healing. St Guerric of Igny, not the most famous of saints, writes,

These clefts, so many open wounds all over his body, offer pardon to the guilty and bestow grace on the just ... For in his loving kindness and compassion he opened his side in order that the blood of the wound might give you life, the warmth of his body revive you, the breath of his heart flow into you as if through a free and open passage.[6]

Our wounding is not a barrier to the grace of God, but rather a means to becoming agents of reconciliation and peace for others. St Guerric reminds us later in the sermon that it is only possible when we realise that our lives are hid with Christ in God (Col. 3:3).

To be in the 'person of Christ' is to be embraced in the Godhead, to be caught up in the self-giving love between Father, Son and Spirit. It is to have our wounds held within the heart of God, and that which God holds he sanctifies and those whom he calls he sends, gently and calmly, to be his ambassadors in a world which has its own wounds and its own need for healing.

There are, of course, risks and fears to face. Jack Dominian, the psychiatrist, writes of the assumption so many make

that psychiatrists, psychiatric nurses, psychologists and social workers either have no problems or that they overcome them. The truth is that the ranks of these workers are full of sensitive, vulnerable people whose formal training in no way eliminates their frailties or problems. Some of them are indeed fortunate in overcoming their individual difficulties, and a combination of learning skills, coupled with their own healed selves, makes them remarkable healers. Others have not managed to overcome their difficulties, or they remain blind to them with no insight and despite their professional skills, they are limited in the help they can offer.[7]

There are a number of fears caught up in this small paragraph. For those who cannot admit their own woundedness, there is the energy used in keeping it hidden even from themselves. Often, in religious circles, such fear reveals itself in a presentation of complete certainty with little room for doubt. It is the equivalent of the consultant who relies only on her medical training. Faced with the trauma of other people's souls, they may find themselves left empty of love, empty of humanity.

For those who are aware of their woundedness but have found no places to express it where they may receive 'unconditional positive regard', there is the constant enervating fear of being discovered. Perhaps the greatest danger to any kind of pastoral work is not the woundedness of those engaged in it, but that woundedness which is not recognised. Better, of course, if the woundedness can be brought into the light in a 'safe' place, to find healing through the deep friendship of others on the journey or, if necessary, with the aid of skilled professionals. Either way, there will be also the healing brought through prayer where God removes the layers and heals us, holding us as we feel the pain of becoming more whole.[8]

Part of the fear, then, is about becoming aware. Another level of fear is that experienced when God has already begun the healing process whereby he strips us so that we depend on him. Sr Kirsty describes this fear perfectly,

I'd be terrified if that happened to me – terrified that when all the skins had been taken away I'd eventually find there was nothing there, just an emptiness . . . Exactly, isn't that the fear of us all, that when all the masks have been removed . . . there will be nothing – the 'existential dread' as Kierkegaard called it?[9]

There can be times when we really wonder whether we can bear any more reality. As T. S. Eliot reminds us, humankind can only bear so much. It feels like enormous risk to allow God to carry on his healing. Again T. S. Eliot catches it in a few words, 'the wounded surgeon plies the steel'.[10] In that is encouragement. The God who is healing us has himself been wounded.

These are some of the fears, and the risks. The risk of going into deep water is that you may not swim, you may look a fool, people may misunderstand and think you are putting yourself forward. There is the risk inherent in Sr Kirsty's fear – the risk that there may be nothing when the layers are gone. There is the risk of disclosing your vulnerability to another. There is also the risk of keeping it hidden where it may fester and erupt in an uncontrolled way or in a setting which is neither safe nor appropriate. There is the risk of speaking your truth, the risk that some will respond positively whilst others confirm their opinion that you are somehow 'odd'.[11] There is the risk of praying, of being open with God – the risk that God will actually hear and 'ply the steel' and that he will use your vulnerability in the healing of others. There is the risk that if you disclose your truth to a person who cannot handle it, both you and they will be damaged and so may your relationship.

We need to distinguish between appropriate and inappropriate risks. Much has already been said about circles of intimacy and degrees of disclosure. The need is for continuous discernment. There is also a need to recognise that God does not invite us to risk ourselves beyond what we are capable of bearing (see 1 Cor. 10:13). Often it is not God calling us to risk, rather that we risk ourselves. We see what others are doing. We admire the callings that others have and we claim that calling for ourselves. In listening to those who are exploring a vocation to ministry there is often a clear distinction between those who have sensed a call over a long time, have resisted it, tried to put it to one side and only then, tentatively, agreed to say 'Yes' to exploring it more; then there are others who almost insist that they have a calling and after the first inspiration have failed to discern the voice of God any further. In doing so people put themselves at enormous risk, for God continually nudges us to listen and to re-adjust our direction as we see fresh insights. It is too easy for the word 'vocation' to be used to define a trajectory of the ego rather than taking the risk of following Christ.

The following of Christ is, in fact, the opposite of certainty. It is the acceptance of uncertainty. It is living by trust rather than certain knowledge. It is following the one who finds himself hung on a cross and who knows what it is to feel forsaken. Perhaps for all of us, that is the greatest risk: when we have followed what we thought was God's leading, when we have shaped our lives according to our insights, insights which have been confirmed in prayer and by those we trust, only to discover ourselves in a situation where we no longer experience consolation. Quite simply, it pays to read the 'health warning' before you follow Christ, and the 'health warning' is written on Golgotha. As we ponder the cross, there is nothing to be gained by being 'soft' about the risks, but before we decide this is not for us we need also to understand why the risks are worth taking.

Vulnerability Motivated by Love

These words say it all. Why else would we follow, except that we know he loves us and we love him. Where else can we go? He has the words of eternal life (John 6:68). In all the feeling of chaos and struggle that the journey may engender, Jesus says, 'Do not be afraid; I AM' (John 6:20). We are drawn by love to look at Jesus, to find in his attractiveness all the motivation we need, to find in him our everything – not a substitute for living and human loving but a fulfilment of all our living and loving; not a pious illusion, but the reality of a living God.

In coming to a knowledge of this Christ who stands among us, he draws us to offer ourselves. In the hiddenness of our journey, the struggle between rebelliousness and surrender will go on, but there is a depth of surrender which is pure gift; a surrender which constrains us with the love of Christ, a surrender which, whatever the seeming chaos of our lives, says 'Yes' in our deepest self. It is discovering that surrender which makes us content to live with change, even with chaos, never being overwhelmed but prepared to sit still and trust, to wait until God reveals his new beginning.

Only love can do this. Only love can take us on the journey from fear to trust. We know that to be true in human terms. So often the wounds of childhood and adolescence are healed quite naturally by the steady, accepting love of a friend or partner. Sometimes it needs more; it needs the training and the appropriate love of professional helpers, and always underlying those loves, recognised or unrecognised, is the healing love of God.

The journey is motivated by love alone. St Ignatius makes that clear in his exercises: that only as we are attracted by the love of Christ can we grow in freedom; only by the strength of our attraction can we dare to let go of our fears and anxieties, our attachments and self-protection and be vulnerable to intimacy with Christ. St John of the Cross invites us too to see our hope in Jesus alone, in nothing else. Often John's teaching can appear bleak, but it is founded on love. John draws us to love only.

> you feel that he loves and does good to you with wisdom
> you feel that he loves you with goodness
> you feel that with holiness and love he favours you
> you feel that in justice and love he favours you
> you feel his mercy, mildness and clemency
> you feel that his love for you is strong, sublime and delicate
> you feel that he loves you in a pure and undefiled way
> he loves you in truthfulness
> he liberally loves and favours you
> he loves you with supreme humility.[12]

and St John of the Cross hears these words from the mouth of God:

I am yours and for you and delighted to be what I am so as to be yours and give myself to you.[13]

It is love which enables us to walk the Christ-way. Nothing else. We need to remind ourselves constantly of that, to listen only to the gentle voice of love. While this book seeks to challenge all who follow Christ, not just those in leadership, to surrender themselves more deeply, it is not a call to be brutal, but only gentle. Especially for those of us to whom life gave little 'basic trust', it is important that the risks we take are the risks God asks us to take, and not those of our own devising to prove ourselves. There is little point in diving in the deep end until you feel at home in the shallows. The mystery and the wonder is that whatever our history, however little basic trust has been instilled by our human experience, God can grant us such a grace – gift, that we can do all that he will ask of us. No more, but certainly no less. Whatever our background, it is in trusting in God's love, whether or not we sense it, that we can dare to become vulnerable for Christ.

Vulnerability as a Voluntary Relinquishment of Power

To choose to relinquish power can have its dangers. In fact it is perhaps more accurate to speak not of relinquishing power but the 'handing over' of power, whether it be to God or to the realities of our life, or to other people who affect us. This 'handing over' has its echoes in the Scriptures.[14]

For Jesus, the handing over is to the power of the Spirit. It is the Spirit of God which takes the Son of God, newly baptised, into the desert. Here is the voluntary relinquishment of power, as Jesus gives himself to be directed by the Spirit into whatever the Father will have him do, and then faces the battering that we too have to face as we endure the battle within between the two Kingdoms, God's and ours. In that battle we discover our true identity, we discover our need of God, we uncover layers of fears and anxieties we never knew existed in us. In other words, should we endure it, we are made stronger, more ourselves, more able to serve God. Though we may have handed power over, we have not in fact handed ourselves over; our 'self' has been renewed through the experience. It is as though in the wilderness experience, God teaches us himself (cf. John 6:45) what trust means. It means handing our life to him and accepting the wounding that follows. Should the wilderness experience have been confined to 40 days it would seem enough, but the reality is, as

St John makes clear by spreading the temptations throughout his Gospel, that the temptations, the hostile response to love, the rejection, poverty and humiliation continue until the surrender is complete. Then love, deep 'primal love', triumphs.

And if the temptations and wounds continue, it is for a purpose; that we might grow in love and be filled with the fullness of God (Eph. 3) and that we might serve him, without knowing the outcome.[15] We are, in this struggle, closer to Christ than we know. We are being granted the privilege not only to believe in him but also to suffer with him.

Time and again the wilderness experience takes people by surprise. Those selected for training for ministry often discover that training is not quite what they expected. They discover that it costs them greatly at a personal level. They feel vulnerabilities being exposed and weaknesses highlighted. Many question what is happening. It is when we see such experiences in the light of the wilderness experience, or in the light of Gethsemane, that we see that handing ourselves over to God, handing ourselves over to the human institution which is the Church, will be wounding as well as healing. Both are necessary if we are to serve the world. We must trust the process.

In the wilderness we will not only discover more about ourselves but more about God once we stop rejecting the experience and see the pattern of Christ in it. The journey into God will take us always a bit further. There is always more, and in the going into the desert with him, as we hear the crashing of the idols, we will come to rely on him more and more, letting go of much that had seemed important but now, with him, seems irrelevant. It takes a lot to trust in this way.

A woman with a terminal illness was told that blood tests confirmed that the disease had developed faster than was expected, that her lungs were weak and that she would have very little time left. That evening she watched a documentary on the television. The film was about white water canoeing. The team of canoeists was being interviewed and one of them was asked 'Are you afraid?' He, looking at the cascading water, the jagged rocks of the enclosing valley, the frailty of his craft, and said, 'Yes, but the only way out is through.'

For the woman and her husband the incident was a cameo of where they were. They had four young children, the hospital was 200 miles from their home and they had only a few days. Were they afraid? Yes, but the only way out was through. If life had already tested them and their faith in the five years of her illness, it was about to test them in their own crucifixion. What carried them through was simply the trust that the water, rough as it was and stormy as it could be, would carry them through and carry them to where God would have them be. They did not pray, not in words. They did not discuss. There was just a silent agreement that they could trust. Reflecting later, the husband realised that the trust stemmed from the simple recognition that through the illness there had already been wilderness experiences, there had already been a Gethsemane, there had already been times of healing. The one word which had sustained them for a long time had been *Emmanuel*, 'God with us'. Somehow they had handed over power long before. It was not even clear when. They knew, independently and together, that they had to relinquish power over the outcome, accept the wounding and see it as a privilege to suffer with Christ. What made it possible was not their faith, which often questioned and experienced anger, despair and isolation, but a gifted faith in the faithfulness of God. This faithful God, who cannot deny himself, who cannot be unfaithful, had somehow brought them this far. They could say 'Yes' to the white water of death and bereavement.

Such trust as this couple experienced in the faithfulness of God is the underlying approach which makes vulnerability possible. In the second part of this book we will suggest how such vulnerability affects crucial areas of the life of the Church, not attempting to give blueprints but rather seeking to indicate possible areas of thought and discussion.

For now, faithfulness and grace must lead us into deeper water.

The natural buoyancy of the water in a swimming bath seems to me a paradigm of the grace of God. It is all around us; it sustains us. But we can resist it – and this resistance may or may not be deliberate. A swimmer can, if he or she wishes, sink to the bottom of the swimming bath – can overcome the natural buoyancy of the water; but a non-swimmer does so unintentionally, by no wish of his or her own. Swimmers insulate themselves from the buoyancy of the water; non-swimmers do so inadvertently by their intense preoccupation with 'doing the right thing' . . . so we may insulate ourselves from the sustenance – the buoyancy – of the grace of God. . .[16]

NOTES

1. Ivan Mann.

2. See Thomas Lane, *A Priesthood in Tune* (Dublin, The Columba Press, 1993) especially Chapters 12 and 13 for a beautiful exploration of what this means for our baptism and for those who are ordained.

3. To explore this theme, see Hans Küng, *On Being a Christian* (Glasgow, Fount, 1978), Section III.2, 'Coping with the negative side'.

4. See Chapter 1.

5. Translated by K. Kavanaugh and O. Rodriguez, *The Collected Works of St John of the Cross* (Washington, ICS Publications, 1991), p. 58. Poem 7: 'Stanzas applied spiritually to Christ and the soul'.

6. St Guerric of Igny, *Liturgical Sermons*: Volume 2 (Spencer, Massachusetts Cistercian Publications, 1971), p. 71. Fourth Sermon for Palm Sunday.

7. Jack Dominian, *Make or Break: An Introduction to Marriage Counselling* (London, SPCK, 1994), p. 9.

8. Of clergy, Jack Dominian writes:

> *If they can overcome their own sensitivities, then their integrated whole selves, coupled with their commitment to Christ, makes them remarkable witnesses. But the clergy need to have continuous insight into themselves and must be prepared to share their own lives with those they are helping, to the extent that such sharing and disclosure is helpful.* (Make or Break, *p. 9*)

9. Sr Kirsty, *The Choice* (London, Hodder & Stoughton, 1982), p. 147.

10. From 'Four Quartets' in T. S. Eliot, *The Complete Poems and Plays* (London, Book Club Associates, 1969), p. 181.

11. This is caught beautifully by Jim Cotter. He writes: 'the courage you have in being vulnerable will sometimes impress and sometimes silence and make thoughtful those who hear.' Jim Cotter, *Revisiting Prayers at Night* (Cairns Publications), pp. 67–8.

12. *The Collected Works of St John of the Cross*, Living Flame 3.6.

13. ibid.

14. See Chapter 7.

15. Charles de Foucauld comes to mind as the obvious example of one who abandoned himself to love and who died without witnessing the full effect of his life and witness.

16. W. H. Vanstone, *Fare Well in Christ* (London, DLT, 1997), p. 88.

Part II

Part II

10

Prophetic Vulnerability:
Professionalism

If we professionalise pastoral care, we will lose the spontaneity and simplicity which characterises love ... [W]e must look ... closely at the nature of the Christian vocation to love and at the strengths and weaknesses of the professional approach.[1]

It is often assumed that those who lead within the Christian community are professionals. Such an assumption is based upon an understanding of what it means to be a professional, and it is an assumption which often carries with it unspoken beliefs about how such a leader ought to behave and to exercise his 'profession'.

This chapter seeks to follow Alistair Campbell's injunction to 'look closely at the Christian vocation to love and at the strengths and weaknesses of the professional approach' – not only in the specific task of pastoral care, but also in the leadership task as a whole. In particular, it seeks to explore whether those who lead in the Christian community really *are* or even *should be* described as professionals, or whether they should simply *be* 'professional'. It asks what, if anything, is distinctive about the professionalism of those who are commissioned to be leaders (whether ordained or lay), and also whether there is any sense in which the vulnerable leadership, of which we have spoken in Part I, and a 'professional' calling to that leadership are compatible.

It will necessarily tend to focus upon those who are recognised as leaders by virtue of ordination and/or stipendiary employment. Nevertheless, many of the principles which emerge during the course of this chapter, in respect of the relationship between professionalism and vulnerability, may be equally applied both to those who exercise an 'un-paid' leadership role within the Christian community, and also to those in other professions who value the insights of the Christian tradition within their own sphere of work.

Was Jesus a Professional?

It is always dangerous to superimpose modern conceptions on to the example and context of Christ as he is depicted in the gospels. Fully aware of the shortcomings of such an exercise, we shall, nevertheless, consider in this chapter the story of the raising of Lazarus in John 11. Why was Jesus there? Simply as a friend, or as a leader with his followers, or as something else? How does Jesus' conduct in that particular crisis match up to what might legitimately have been expected of him? Did he handle the situation well, or did he act in any way inappropriately? Was Jesus a professional? (This exercise is not setting out to affirm or condemn contemporary professional practice, but merely to act as a mirror to that practice and, in so doing, to raise some pertinent questions about it in relation to leadership within the Christian context.)

In order to answer the question 'Was Jesus a professional?', it is first necessary to outline what we might mean by the term. Alastair Campbell, who has written extensively on the relation between professionalism and pastoral care (and to whom we are particularly indebted in this chapter), points out that originally the term 'profession' referred to 'the public declaration of faith associated with a life of religious obedience',[2] so perhaps it is ironic that it should be necessary to ask questions concerning the 'professional' status of Christian leaders at all! Others, such as Anthony Russell,[3] have clearly traced the development of the term and its application (albeit uncomfortably at times) to the ordained clergy, as well as to particular career groups (such as the law and medicine), and eventually to a particular socio-economic class, the members of which have developed characteristic ways of working.

It is these characteristics which gave the terms 'professional' and 'professionalism' their substance. James Glasse[4] suggested five basic characteristics of professionalism, to which others may be added. These are:

(i) education
(ii) expertise
(iii) dedication
(iv) responsibility
(v) relationship to an institution

The first two point to some form of specialist training and the acquisition of knowledge and skills, often in specialist institutions, with their own methods of examination, certification and 'ritual' initiation. The third characteristic points to some altruistic motive for the service offered (although this is sometimes questionable, since the financial and status 'returns' of most professions is relatively high!). The fourth and fifth characteristic points to an accountability both to the client and the parent institution which carries ethical obligations and the potential for disciplinary action.

The rise of professionalism has had a significant effect on our perceptions of Christian leadership. As more and more professions emerged during the eighteenth, nineteenth and twentieth centuries, areas of professional work and expertise narrowed into distinct specialisms. This had a profound effect on the clergyman's role and the clergy came to be 'technologists of the sanctuary'.[5] To some extent in reaction to this, and as a result of changing social patterns, such as greater urbanisation, the clergy began to model themselves on other professions by developing practitioner/client relationships, thus shifting the emphasis of their pastoral care and leadership to the *individual* rather than to the community as a whole. Nevertheless, the clergy never attained the same degree of professionalisation as other high-status occupational groups, due, in part, to the long-standing and continuing effects of patronage and the established status of the Church.

So it is that modern Western society has come to associate the professional with knowledge, training, discipline and ethical conduct, as one who deals with vulnerable people in a trustworthy, competent, controlled and emotionally neutral way.[6] This 'control' is particularly evident in those professions which have to deal repeatedly with distressing situations: for example, police and ambulance crews dealing with road traffic accidents; pathologists handling mutilated bodies with clinical detachment; social workers and doctors entering into situations of squalor and degradation without expressing judgement or disgust. Such 'control' creates a distance and detachment which can both isolate and insulate the professional from the person. The professional's own stress is either ignored or subdued, and empathy becomes a technique for 'getting through' a difficult situation in a safe way. Expressed care becomes a veneer for emotional neutrality. The client becomes a case or a type, and the individuality of both parties – carer and cared for – is lost.

To view Jesus' conduct in John 11 in the light of the characteristics of professionalism which we have just outlined is – to say the least – interesting! Suffice it to say that if he was being observed by a training supervisor, he might possibly be invited to think again about his chosen career! As we suggested above, it is a limited exercise. Nevertheless, it does reveal some surprising, even shocking, contrasts between Jesus' handling of a critical pastoral situation, and what might be expected of a professional Christian leader today.[7]

Firstly, Jesus was 'untrained'. His knowledge and expertise came in the form of a natural 'gifting' in relating to people and a unique sensitivity to the prompting of the Holy Spirit. The account given by Luke of Jesus' conversation with the teachers in the Temple (4:46f) is a clear indication of his depth of knowledge (even at the age of twelve), some of which he would no doubt have acquired via the 'human' teaching within the family/community setting. This encounter with the teachers in the Temple could be understood in terms of an 'examination', and his likely initiation into adulthood as a form of 'certification'. His true 'ritual' initiation for ministry, however, was surely his baptism by John – the culmination of thirty years of 'hidden' formation. Clearly, by the time he came to the crisis of Lazarus' death, Jesus had acquired considerable experience in dealing with both individuals and crowds, and had successfully raised two other persons from the dead: the son of the widow of Nain (Luke 7:11–17) and Jairus' daughter (Matt. 9:18–26 cf. Mark 5:21–43; Luke 8:40–56). Yet the fact remains that he was untrained for his work.

Was he dedicated to the task of raising Lazarus? Undoubtedly, yes, but it is clear from the passage that there was an ulterior motive. He loved Lazarus, and he loved Martha and Mary (John 11:5), and for that reason wanted his friend to come back to life; but the real motive for this miracle was 'for God's glory, so that the Son of God may be glorified through it' (John 11:4 cf. v.15). Such a statement hardly sounds like altruism! It is true that the miracle would also benefit the crowd (v.42), but Jesus could, justifiably, be accused of manipulating the situation for his own ends (just as Martha, Mary and the crowd could be accused of manipulating it for theirs! See vv.21, 32 and 37).

Several things in this passage may be noted which might suggest that Jesus acted irresponsibly, even unethically. Firstly, there is the slowness of his response to the cry for help (v.6), a delay which seems to persist even longer (vv.29–30). It is true, as we pointed out in Chapter 7,[8] that it is not always appropriate to respond immediately to a cry for help. Nevertheless, the deliberate ignoring of a call to attend to a dying man would seem odd, if not uncaring, were it to happen today. Jesus himself may well have known that Lazarus would live, but that knowledge offered little comfort to the anguished sisters, miles away in Bethany, despite Westcott's comment that 'because the Lord loved the family, He went at the exact moment when His visit would be most fruitful, and not just when He was invited'.[9]

Secondly, he puts himself and his disciples at risk by choosing to travel through a part of the country where he had already been threatened with stoning (vv.7ff). Thirdly, he is less than clear in his conversation with the disciples, speaking in euphemisms about Lazarus' death (vv.11f). Fourthly, his relating to the two sisters is questionable. It is true that he knew them already (cf. v.2. Also Luke 10:38–42) and that he did listen to their pleas (vv.21f, v.32), but he could also be accused of allowing himself to be hero-worshipped (v.32) and of not setting appropriate boundaries within which his conversations with the women could take place. The conversation with Martha may have taken place in private but that with Mary certainly did not! (v.33a). Lastly, his actions at the tomb were irresponsible in the extreme. His public instruction to open the tomb prompted a spectacle which was not only potentially harrowing for the two sisters and the crowd of mourners but also a health hazard (v.39). Professionally speaking, Jesus' conduct at the scene of crisis was a disaster!

What is worse is that he was not accountable for that conduct to any *human* institution, but only to his heavenly Father. He does not, therefore, respond to the taunting accusations made about him (v.37) or bother to justify the way he has behaved. Rather, he is a maverick in splendid isolation! Nevertheless, the 'institution' which may have felt responsible for dealing with his actions (the chief priests and the Pharisees) decide to take action against him (vv.47–53). He must be silenced.

What of the other characteristics of professionalism? Was Jesus trustworthy and competent? In terms of results, his ministry was certainly effective, and it is clear that Mary and Martha, the disciples and the crowd all trusted him; he did, after all, ask them to do some extraordinary things! His ministry was to all of them, not just to the sisters. In that sense, he resembles more the 'pre-professional' ministry of the Christian leader to the whole community rather than the more individual 'client-centred' approach.

Yet what is most striking about Jesus' conduct in this crisis is his own reactions to it. Here is no controlled, emotionally neutral, detached handling of a difficult situation. Here is no empathetic 'veneer' of caring. No, here the Son of God enters deeply into the pain of the death of a friend, the sorrow of the sisters and the mourning of the crowd – *despite the fact that he knew Lazarus would rise again* (vv.4, 23). He stood in solidarity alongside the mourners and identified with them in an overt way. Westcott, in his commentary on the passage, suggests:

the miracles of the Lord were not wrought by the simple word of power, but . . . in a mysterious way the element of sympathy entered into them. He took away the sufferings and diseases of men in some sense by taking them upon himself.[10]

Jesus' own expression of his distress (vv.33, 35, 38) – whatever its cause – would certainly not be considered to be the appropriate behaviour of a professional. Grayston comments:

[The disciples] expected to see people mourning, as indeed they did; but they also saw an extraordinary outbreak of emotion by Jesus – tears which could e read as signs of love, deep inward distress, and even indignation.[11]

This solidarity and identification which is not afraid to express its own anguish and pain stands in striking contrast to most 'professional' caring. Over-identification and emotional involvement with clients leads to loss of impartiality, loss of accepted codes of behaviour and eventually a loss of the ability to help. It is true that in this instance, the carer, Jesus, knew the family well. Indeed, there was, in the relationship, already a mutuality of caring (cf. Luke 10:38f and John 12:1–8), but surely such a public outpouring of emotion would be deemed unacceptable for today's 'professional' Christian leaders? Christopher Moody disagrees:

God himself is not uninvolved . . . He is as warmly involved as is a nomadic shepherd with his sheep. He totally identifies himself with the needs of his people . . . If God's behaviour is not . . . impartial, but based on a passionate identification with his people, then the same is expected of the leaders he appoints over them.[12]

It is clear from our observations above that Jesus was not (in the modern sense) a 'professional'. It is true that he had knowledge and skills, both naturally and spiritually imparted, but he was neither detached from those he led and cared for, nor emotionally neutral. This passage, and the gospels as a whole, reveal rather a leader who accompanied his followers, was motivated only by love, who expressed anger, tears, frustration and pain, and who accompanied those who followed him, risked standing alongside people, shared their pain and brought healing and hope.

In many ways, Jesus resembles more the original usage of the term 'professional' – as one who makes a 'public declaration of faith associated with a life of religious obedience' (see p. 104 above). As we have seen, his motive was to give glory to God through the miracle of raising Lazarus, and so open people's eyes to who *he* was (vv.4, 15, 23–7, 40–3). In that sense, at least, he 'professed' the faith. Thus, in Jesus' ministry, evangelism and pastoral care went together, and it was, in part, as he expressed his *own* distress and anguish that people's eyes were opened to who he was and where he had come from (John 11:42).[13]

'See how he loved him' (John 11:36)

Jesus took the risk of expressing love and, as he did so, he provoked a mixed response. Many believed (v.45); others criticised (v.37). Yet it was this element of love – expressed in all its depth and pain – which prevented Jesus' ministry at the grave of Lazarus from simply being a spectacular demonstration of supernatural power. Love earthed his actions in human living and human relating with particular persons.

This dialectic between power and love is at the heart of the issue of professionalism for the Christian leader. For to be a professional is to exercise power, and often to exercise power over vulnerable people. As we noted in Chapter 5, power is not intrinsically evil; it is how it is used that matters. Nouwen observes that much Christian leadership displays 'a desire to control complex situations, confused emotions and anxious minds'.[14]

By contrast, Richard Holloway points out that Christ's mission was one of 'reversal':

He reversed all the world's hierarchies in his own nature. As the divine Word he overturned human expectations of the powerful by his great act of divine self-emptying. And this law of kenosis ruled his conduct. . . The great challenge for Christians is to . . . learn how to de-egotize leadership, to find a model of kenotic leadership which leads for the sake of truth, for the sake of love, and not for any more complicated inner motive to do with the satisfaction of the exercise of power itself.[15]

Love, then, must be at the heart of Christian leadership. Campbell identifies '*agape* love' as the distinguishing factor of the Christian vocation and of Christian professionalism. Compared with 'moderated love' – the term he uses to describe the consistent professional caring of, for example, doctors, nurses and social workers – he sees *agape* love as even more demanding:

the love which risks self in order to enhance values [in the other]. . . Agape requires that no help, however well-intentioned, should stamp out one's own or another's individuality.[16]

For the Christian leader is not called to care in a general way, but rather is led by the Spirit to minister to each person in a particular way. For some, that ministry will be to offer strength, reliability, nurture and support; for others, the Spirit may require a willingness to minister out of weakness and vulnerability, offering identification, companionship and a sharing in pain. Indeed, the vocation to love in this way cannot be separated from suffering:

When it comes to a knowledge of persons which genuinely seeks to help them, there can be no knowledge without pain. This is arguably what is most distinctive about the Christian gospel . . . [T]he Christian meaning of love is . . . not the offering of a victim to appease a distant deity, but a love which identified totally with the most despised and rejected of human beings. . . The Cross . . . is the revelation of love as involvement. . . Even an omniscient God must share our flesh to know us in love's way.[17]

It is this willingness to enter into 'love as involvement', with all the risks it carries, which sets Christian professional leaders apart from others. For to do so flies in the face of recommended professional practice, and makes them vulnerable both to the 'client' and the 'institution'. It takes away their protected status and opens them up to misunderstanding and rejection from both directions.[18]

But how can the Christian leader be true to this vocation to love and remain credible as a 'professional' leader in the community? Is the clerical profession different to all others, and should it be?[19] When that question was asked of an active clergyman recently, he replied: 'I don't think of myself as a professional, but I hope I act professionally.' What he seemed to be saying was that he values and affirms much that characterises professional conduct generally, *but he does not wish to be constrained by it.* He wants to be free to respond openly, to get 'too involved' from time to time, to go against recommended practice, to risk getting it wrong, if that is how he believes the Holy Spirit is prompting him, and if that is how he believes he most effectively incarnates the love of God for the people he is there to serve.

This is the point at which leaders who choose to walk the way of vulnerability become prophetic in their ministries, with all the loneliness and risk which the prophetic role can bring. It is costly not only for them but also for the family, congregation and the wider establishment of which they may be representatives. We have suggested already that vulnerability can both attract and alienate; that it can bring pain as well as growth, misunderstanding as well as benefits and challenge to others. For a leader to take the risk of expressing her own emotional responses, and being honest about her own weakness, can lead to accusations of unprofessional conduct, incompetence and rejection. Occasionally, however, such openness may have the opposite effect, encouraging a sense of 'reality' and 'humanness' about the Church, and making it more approachable. When Jesus wept at the tomb of Lazarus, people were moved either to compassion or to anger: it should not surprise us that however 'professional' her conduct in other ways, a Christian leader's tears may do the same.

Being Professional or Professional Being?

So far in this chapter our emphasis has been on the distinctiveness of the Christian vocation to love, and on the fact that the Christian leader cannot be true to his calling without sometimes 'sitting light' to the rules of professionalism. Now is the time to redress the balance somewhat, for the strengths of the professional approach for the Christian leader are many, if some of the pitfalls of leadership are to be avoided.

For example, the establishment and maintenance of boundaries (whether spatial, temporal, physical or concerning information or knowledge) continues to be of perennial importance for those in leadership. For boundaries set limits which exist to create freedom to relate within those limits rather than to prevent relating. John Bowker has suggested that 'we live within boundaries of constraint which delimit the possibilities of what we can do'.[20]

This is not a *negative* observation, but rather a liberating one. Boundaries which are chosen, and constraints (whether chosen or not), provide security and help to maintain what the caring professions might describe as a 'critical distance' in pastoral care. The wisdom and value of such an empathetic approach cannot be under-estimated.[21] Nevertheless it sits uncomfortably with the notion of God who, in Christ, became intimately involved with humanity and who, through the Holy Spirit, fruitfully identified with and ministered to them. The incarnate Son of God did not maintain a critical distance from humanity but was prepared to enter fully into the human condition with all its suffering and pain. That he was able to do so depended not only on his relationship with his Father through the Spirit, made particularly evident at key moments in his ministry and maintained through his life of prayer, but also on his relationship with those around him. This was what freed him to take the risk of crossing boundaries, becoming deeply involved and daring to love.

Boundaries *are* important, but from time to time Christian leaders may similarly be called to cross them. When they do, their own needs and weakness may be revealed and they will need the support and prayers of others. Just as other professions depend on the support of a network of supervision, so it is at this point that a spiritual director or companion – someone who offers the 'unconditional positive regard' of which we spoke in Part I – becomes vital for the Christian leader. For it takes courage for a 'professional' to 'rejoice with those who rejoice and weep with those who weep', and it depends on prayer.

A professional approach to Christian leadership will also keep leaders alert to the dangers of manipulation, lack of accountability and isolation from other professionals. It will provide a more secure environment both for the leader and those whom she serves, and it will safeguard against the danger of the abuse of power. Being *pro-fessional*, if not being *a professional*, is vital for Christians in leadership.

There is, however, another side to the coin. Rather than *being* professional, it is perhaps best described as professional *being*. In our explorations into the vulnerability of prayer and of waiting in Part I, we spoke of the demanding task of 'passive activity': the choosing simply to be and allow others to do to you rather than to take action towards them. It is about being present whatever the consequences. The temptation for those in the caring professions, as well as

Christian leaders, is always to be doing something or saying something, to offer comfort, help or advice. Professional *being*, being there alongside another in his pain, is one of the most demanding forms of offering care. Such companionship shares bodily presence, but does not impose or demand any response. It is about silence and waiting and powerlessness, and it emphasises the vulnerability of love:

The love Jesus offers to the poor, the outcast and the disabled is tangible in quality. There is . . . a being there, a fearless and restorative presence. . . Love is presence, or it is nothing but empty form.[22]

Those who choose to walk the way of vulnerability will soon discover that it is in the *being* – being who they are (even if that breaks the professional rules) and being with others in their joy and in their pain – that Christian leaders must sometimes stand slightly 'outside' professionalism as it is normally understood. As they make that discovery, they will find themselves walking in the steps of the incarnate Son of God.

Enabling others to learn to be, and to combine the Christian vocation to love with the strengths of the professional approach, is the demanding task of those with responsibility for the training and formation of leaders. It is to this that we now turn.

> *Let the minister of God approve himself not only in the outward display of professional kindliness, but in the inward unfeigned love of the heart.*[23]

NOTES

1. A. V. Campbell, *Paid to Care? The Limits of Professionalism in Pastoral Care* (London, SPCK, 1985), p. 4.
2. ibid., p. 10.
3. Anthony Russell, *The Clerical Profession* (London, SPCK, 1980).
4. James Glasse, *Profession: Minister* (Oxford, Abingdon Press, 1969).
5. Russell, p. 40.

6. Russell, p. 253:

> *A professional man in the twentieth century is characteristically a man of high and certified competence in a defined area of knowledge in which he is an expert.*

7. Although John 11 depicts, primarily, a pastoral crisis, it would be possible to undertake a similar exercise in respect of other passages from Scripture which reveal Jesus exercising his leadership role (e.g. his teaching ministry and feeding of the five thousand; his handling of the Last Supper and events of the Passion).

8. See p. 80.

9. B. F. Westcott, *The Gospel according to St John* (London, John Murray, n.d.), p. 82.

10. ibid., p. 96.

11. K. Grayston, *The Gospel of John* (London, Epworth, 1990), p. 92.

12. Christopher Moody, *Eccentric Ministry: Pastoral Care and Leadership in the Parish* (London, DLT, 1992), p. 22.

13. Moody suggests that clerical professionalism has, in fact, *hindered* evangelism, causing clergy to focus inwardly on their congregations rather than outwardly to the world. Due to their lack of confidence in the professional world *beyond* their church walls, leaders have become pre-occupied with maintenance rather than mission. He suggests:

> *We need to ... ask how the Church can be re-orientated once again ... In the process, the clergy may have to surrender their hard-won sense of professional identity in favour of a more open negotiation with the expectations of people inside and outside the Church. It may be that their professionalism is one of the major obstacles preventing a more responsive and mission-orientated ministry from the Church as a whole. (p. 58)*

14. Henri Nouwen, *In the Name of Jesus: Reflections on Christian Leadership* (London, DLT, 1989), p. 56.

15. Richard Holloway (ed.), *The Divine Risk* (London, DLT, 1990), pp. xv–xvi.

16. A. V. Campbell, *Moderated Love: A Theology of Pastoral Care* (London, SPCK, 1984), pp. 82–3.

17. ibid. pp. 89–90.

18. cf. Campbell, *Paid to Care?* (p. 92):

> *The Christian message contains a major challenge to all naive optimism about the way in which love can find root in human life. Nothing can take away from the tragedy at the heart of the Christian gospel, that an innocent and wholly loving man was crucified by the authorities of his day. His followers dare not hope for an easier way to give love a living and active place in human history.*

19. cf. Wesley Carr, *The Priestlike Task: A Model for Developing and Training the Church's Ministry* (London, SPCK, 1985), p. 38: '['Professional'] is not a description which is lightly accepted in the church and some argue that its use alone indicates a mistaken development ...'

20. John Bowker, *A Year to Live* (London, SPCK, 1991), pp. 1–2.

21. Alastair Campbell summarises:

> *a critical distance is required between the helper and the person helped – too great a distance prevents the helper from responding to the other's need: too little*

distance disables the helper from seeing the problem objectively and offering support from outside the situation. (Moderated Love, *p. 81*)

22. Campbell, *Paid to Care?*, p. 99.
23. Canon W. C. E. Newbolt quoted in J. H. L. Morrell (ed.), *The Heart of a Priest: Selections from the writings of W. C. E. Newbolt* (London, SPCK, 1958).

11

Prophetic Vulnerability: Ministerial Formation[1]

Formation in the mind of Christ, who did not cling to power but emptied himself, taking the form of a slave, is not what most seminaries are about.[2]

'Formation in the mind of Christ' is a fundamental vocation for all Christians. 'Becoming like Jesus', 'growing into Christ', 'putting on Christ' – however we like to describe it – is the goal and pattern for all who choose to follow him. We have seen in Part I how (following Christ's example) a chosen vulnerability may sometimes be part of that calling. This chapter will focus specifically on what it means to be 'formed in the mind of Christ' for those who are called to a leadership role within the life of the Christian community, and, in particular, how they are trained for that role. It will explore what we mean by 'ministerial formation' and also some of the tensions between *being trained* and *learning vulnerability*. Reflecting on biblical insights, it will comment on the various contexts for training, and ask whether academic, pastoral and spiritual growth can be held in appropriate balance, or whether (in some instances) 'training' actually militates against personal spiritual formation, and the place of vulnerability within that formation.

What is Ministerial Formation?

Ministerial formation is *a shaping of life for ministry*. It is dynamic, changing, growing. Its purpose is to serve others. It is not so much about qualifications as about life itself; not so much about theological education (although it *is* about that), as about spiritual formation and an equipping to serve others by the grace of God, as much as by the skill of mind or hand. It is 'a formation to live – not a formation to do something in your head'.[3] Kenneth Leech has described it as:

a process in which we are formed by, and in Christ . . . a process of Christening, of being clothed with Christ, and in the process we are transformed. It is a process which involves confrontation, exploration and struggle, and its goal is maturity in Christ.[4]

It is not an easy path to follow, but it is one which cannot be avoided by those who seek to serve and be imitators of the self-emptying Son of God. Leech goes on: 'It is a road which passes through storms and desert wastes, through fire and flood, a road traversed by monsters and demons; a road fraught with danger.'[5] You cannot, therefore, speak of ministerial formation without recognising that vulnerability is or *should be* part of it. Learning appropriate vulnerability, and recognising its creative potential – not only for the vulnerable person but also for those around him – is surely part of what it means to 'grow into Christ'. Yet so much of the ministerial formation of those who are trained to be leaders in the Christian community seems to be about acquiring the means to *prevent* vulnerability and to protect those who lead – and those *whom* they lead – from that 'confrontation, exploration and struggle' which is intrinsic to it.

What is Ministerial Formation for Those in Training for (Ordained) Leadership?

The Advisory Board for Ministry of the Church of England recognises the lifelong process of ministerial formation, suggesting that initial training (for the ordained ministry) should be but 'part of a continuing process of ministerial formation and development',[6] and in its criteria for theological colleges, it speaks of the necessity of 'Effective provision of pastoral care, spiritual development and ministerial formation for ordinands'.[7] In addition, in an Appendix entitled 'Educational Developments in Training for the Ordained Ministry', it lists as number (v) of 'Priorities and Emphases in Theological

Training': '(v) Emphasis can also be given to the student's growth in prayer and spiritual life.'

The Church of England therefore recognises the need to address ministerial formation as part of its task in training ordinands. It must be said, however, that it sometimes comes across as a somewhat 'hidden' and 'optional' priority in a document which focuses largely on an assessment of the academic and technical aspects of training and the effectiveness of their provision through theological colleges and courses.

There are, we suggest, two key factors in assessing what ministerial formation means or *should mean* for those in training for leadership:

(i)   an examination of the distinction between *learning, education* and *training*;

(ii) an examination of the relationship between *knowledge, technique, reflection* and *prayer*.

For whilst such terms can never be held in isolation from each other, a greater understanding of what we mean by each may help us to recognise the necessity for something of a shift in the balance of emphasis in theological training.

Learning has been defined as 'a more or less permanent change of behaviour which is as a result of experience'.[8] It is something which goes on throughout life, whether it is recognised or not. It is broader than *education* or *training*, but encompasses both.[9] The word education comes from the Latin *educare*, 'to lead forth'. The task of the teacher is, therefore, to give information which encourages the student to 'come forth', to emerge, to be set free to serve. *Training* is about the passing on of specific skills and techniques which enable the tasks of leadership.

Ministerial formation is, then, more akin to learning than to education or training, but because it is more difficult to measure or assess when it comes to preparing leaders for ministry, it tends to be sidelined in favour of the other two. Kenneth Leech speaks out strongly of the need to keep all three in balance:

We need to be more concerned with sanctity than with the acquisition of pastoral skills and expertise... We need to recover a view of ministry which stresses the sacramental, charismatic, theological and prophetic roles more than the professional, managerial and organisational ones.[10]

and Allan adds:

Theological training is more than plugging gaps. It helps an ordinand grow in personal knowledge, and that means becoming aware of weakness as well as developing strengths.[11]

Knowledge, in terms of academic study, and the acquisition of skills in, for example, pastoral counselling and leading worship, are vital; but so too is the developing of an ability to reflect theologically on what has been studied and practised, and the encouragement to root that reflection on experience in a carefully nurtured life of prayer. Without reflection and prayer, the acquisition of knowledge and skills can lead to inappropriate, domineering leadership by those too 'young in the faith' to convey the truths and carry the responsibilities which they have been given with integrity.[12] The foundation is, somehow, missing.

Whilst, as we have already emphasised, ministerial formation is a lifelong process, the period of time set apart to 'train' leaders for the Christian community is, nevertheless, crucial in setting patterns for their academic, pastoral and spiritual development throughout their lives. If the spiritual dimension is neglected at *this* stage, then it is possible it will be neglected later. If it is acknowledged and addressed, then the foundations will have been laid for future growth and development.

How, then, can the balance be maintained, and how can a willingness to choose to walk the way of vulnerability – such a vital part of ministerial formation – be encouraged in those who have been called to follow the self-emptying Christ? In short, is 'learning vulnerability' a necessary part of ministerial formation?

Learning Vulnerability: the tensions

When a person becomes an ordinand or trainee minister, and is required to undergo a period of preparation for that leadership role, a number of tensions may arise. How he or she is helped to handle those tensions and grow through them is an important element of their ministerial formation. The tensions themselves will vary according to the context of the training and the previous experience, maturity and family circumstances of the individual. Generally, however, the period of training is one of transition, of change, of leaving behind previous patterns and securities and of having to find new ones.

Very often, the excitement and newness of the period of preparation masks (initially at least) a sense of severe unease and vulnerability in a strange and threatening environment. Often bereft of home, friends, family, previous career and previously recognised lay ministry, the full-time trainee minister can be effectively powerless in an alien institution, required to 'fit in' to particular and sometimes inconvenient patterns of work and worship, with no guarantee of a job at the end of training. For a job will depend on satisfactory completion of that training and on the positive assessment of those who hold responsibility for it. It is a vulnerable place to be.

The question is whether that vulnerability can safely be acknowledged, or whether it remains hidden. Many ordinands speak of the difficulty of acknowledging their uncertainties and struggles because of the false expectations and pressures (real or imagined) which they perceive around them: the false expectation that as trainee 'professional' Christian leaders they will be 'a cut above' the rest, able to handle any personal crisis because of their deep and secure trust in God; the impression that everybody around them is coping wonderfully well, and that they must therefore be weak and odd if they feel that they are not; the fear that to admit to tutors (or even fellow-students) that all is *not* well, will lessen their chances of getting through the course and being ordained or commissioned at the end of it.

Such fears and anxieties are, of course, natural, and are to be expected. What is perhaps surprising is the difficulty which many 'trainees' have in expressing them, working through them creatively, and being supported as they do so. Why should this be so? In theory at least, the structures are in place (usually in the form of a personal tutor) for trainee ministers to find the support and encouragement they need in their personal and spiritual development, alongside their growth in things academic and pastoral. In practice, however, many ordinands do not feel able to utilise these structures, either because they do not trust the tutor concerned,[13] or (more likely) because the overall, prevailing ethos of their period of training is one of *adding on*, of being equipped, and getting ready – an ethos which militates against any admission of weakness, inability and hesitation. It is often only in severe personal crisis (when it is no longer possible to hide) that a trainee minister will reveal his vulnerability. Ironically, it is often through such personal crisis that true ministerial formation takes place.

Ministerial formation should not, however, be simply the product of personal crisis, but should be integral, even fundamental to any preparation for a leadership role within the Christian community. The serious question is how that task is being addressed in a positive and creative way by those with responsibility for training, and how the ethos of training may become one where it is understood and accepted as integral. It is a matter of both *making space* for such formation to take place, and also of ordinands and trainee ministers being encouraged to *take responsibility* for that formation in themselves. It is all too easy, for example, for time and space set aside for quiet to be filled with essay-writing!

It is, of course, impossible to ensure that all theological educators will also be effective pastoral tutors. It is equally impossible to ensure that, if they were, their tutees would trust them sufficiently to express their needs and weaknesses.[14] It is, however, possible to articulate more clearly the place of ministerial formation within the training process: to give public permission for ordinands to fail, to have personal crises, to make mistakes – even to suggest that *not* to do so may be the greater weakness! The sooner we dispel the 'myth of perfection' which pervades many of our training institutions, the sooner those in training will be freed to grow into Christian maturity! Such a plea is, of course, exaggerated: it is, nevertheless, a genuine one.

In practice ministerial formation no longer seems to be a priority in many colleges and courses. This sense of loss is aggravated by the necessary and laudable rise in expectations of the academic and 'technical' elements of ministerial training. It is not insignificant that of fourteen (Anglican) residential theological colleges in existence in 1992 only three specifically mentioned 'ministerial formation' as part of their purpose and aims: of those three, one has now closed, and another avoided closure only because of significant financial support from a private source. In addition, the Aston Training Course, which explicitly sought to 'provide the guidance to enable [students] to develop in their personal life, to work through disabling experiences and to gain self-confidence and greater personal integration'[15] has also now been closed.

Most colleges and courses do, of course, provide personal tutors or chaplains for their students but, despite the ACCM recommendation

4. That each student should have regular meetings with a pastoral or personal tutor or chaplain, to review personal and ministerial development as well as spiritual formation[16]

this aspect often appears, in practice, to be secondary – both in terms of time allocated and emphasis given – to the academic and practical demands of training.

Training as 'Adding on' or 'Letting go'? 'Being ready' or 'Being transparent'?

The tendency to 'professionalise' Christian leadership has encouraged an understanding of training in terms of 'adding on', in the sense of the provision of knowledge and skills which will enable the trainee to undertake the tasks of his profession. Laudable as such an understanding of training is, it is not, as we have already suggested, the whole story, for part of the training of leaders in the Christian community is that they should learn to 'let go'. Put simply, it is a recognition of the 'God-dimension' in the work that they do. However well-equipped in terms of knowledge and skills, they cannot truly minister unless the Spirit of God works through them.[17] For that to happen, there must be a 'letting go' – which is not to suggest that knowledge and skills are abandoned in favour of an irresponsible, *laissez-faire*, attitude, but rather that the humanly acquired (and God-given!) knowledge and skills be offered back, let go of, in order that the Spirit may work with them and through them. If they are *not* abandoned in this way, *they* (rather than God himself) may become the foundation for ministry and leadership.

It is difficult to teach this 'letting go' in an academic institution unless it is somehow modelled and experienced. If the prevailing emphasis is on *ability* and *capability,* and there is little space for inability and struggle, then 'letting go' will be extremely hard (if not impossible) for the reasons we have outlined above. If, on the other hand, students (and even staff) sometimes allow their weakness and vulnerability to be seen, then a recognition of ministerial formation as integral to training may be enhanced. It is simply a case of putting the 'God-dimension' back into the person, and avoiding the danger of creating an impersonal professionalism. It is a transition from a search for *competence* to knowing *confidence* (literally 'with faith'), and so through to 'competent confidence'. Thomas Merton put it this way:

To form . . . is then to draw out the inner spiritual form implanted in [the disciple's] soul by grace: to educate, that is to 'bring out' Christ in him. It is not a matter of imposing . . . a rigid and artificial form from without but to encourage the growth of life and the radiation of light within the soul, until this life and light gain possession of his whole being, inform all his actions with grace and liberty, and bear witness to Christ living in him. It takes account of the whole man called to find his place in the whole Christ.[18]

How many theological training institutions would include that paragraph in their prospectus?

It is, of course, a question of balance. Trainee ministers must be prepared and equipped for ministry; but we need also to nurture in them a transparency to the ministry of *Christ,* rather than over-loading them with information and technique! For if the equipping somehow smothers the Christ within, then something precious and vital has been lost. And 'the Christ within' chose to be vulnerable – some of the time.

This principle of 'letting go' is seen in Jesus' instructions to his own disciples as he prepared to send them out to preach the good news and to heal the sick. At their 'call', they left everything and followed him (Luke 5:11, 28), and in their commissioning they are instructed to 'Take nothing' (Luke 9:3 cf 10:4). They will be vulnerable

(Luke 10:3), but God will work through *them* (Luke 10:17ff) rather than through the wise (Luke 10:21).[19]

Learning to be vulnerable is not easy, especially when to risk doing so is or appears to be to move in the opposite direction to a training ethos whose emphasis seems to be heavily weighted against it. If, however, vulnerability and ministerial formation are closely allied (as we have suggested they are), then it may be through the sensitive and appropriate exercise of a chosen vulnerability, by students and staff alike, that the balance of training within our theological institutions may be redressed, and an over-emphasis on the academic and practical (to the detriment of the spiritual) may be countered.

Learning Vulnerability: the context

We have argued in Part I that a chosen vulnerability is only possible in a relational context.[20] It is important, therefore, to look at the contexts within which Christian leaders are trained and to see whether they are conducive to ministerial formation and the vulnerability which may be part of that formation.

Residence in an institution, or as a significant part of a non-residential course, has been recognised as an important element of training. Quoting from the ACCM Occasional Paper 'Residence: An Education', the 1992 Report to the House of Bishops, *Theological Training: A Way Ahead*, states:

ACCM Council accepted the view of the Working Party that 'residence' was a powerful instrument for the training of the Church's ministers, particularly in relation to ministerial formation through worship, prayer and personal development. (p. 37)

In addition, the 'Paper from the Principals of Theological Colleges' which forms an Appendix to the same Report comments:

The years of training are life-changing as well as informational... By being in the larger community an individual has to come to terms with personal strengths and weaknesses in ministry... (pp. 157f)

One of the key benefits of a residential training is that it creates the potential for the development of the trusting relationships which facilitate ministerial formation and which make a chosen vulnerability possible. The importance of a supportive community in ministerial formation cannot be underestimated.

Yet, as we have already shown, relationships in such a context are not always ideal, either between staff and students or amongst the students themselves, and a positive context for formation cannot be assumed. Sometimes the residential environment is over-intense, so that if members of the community either admit to or are perceived to be in some difficulty, then they run the risk of being 'pounced upon', not only by their tutors but by the entire community who – shut away from the world – are desperate to offer help! Respecting the particularity and, indeed, the *privacy* of a vulnerable member is vital in this instance. It is far too easy for the institutional community to smother – even manipulate and abuse – the one who is, or is perceived to be, in need. 'Great Christian love' can sometimes become a facade for interference and imposition. Help from outside the residential community is often what is needed, and is more often effective. One ordinand commented,

You cannot hide anything in a community like this. Indeed, there is an expectation that you should not hide anything! And if you do, people project on to you what *they* would be feeling, and assume that you feel the same.

For all its benefits, then, a residential training has its negative side. In this context, as much as any other, discernment is vital if a member of the staff or student body is to allow themselves to be vulnerable. Yet, as we have seen, such discernment is built upon, and emerges from, a foundation of prayer – and if that is missing, or neglected, then a chosen vulnerability becomes, at best, extremely risky and, at worst, impossible.

Training courses, where the residential element is a significant but limited part of the course, provide a different context for learning vulnerability. They have a disadvantage in that it may take longer for relationships to gel and for trust to develop, but an advantage in that training is still very much rooted in the 'real world', and the over-intensity of the residential environment may be avoided. It is likely also that those in part-time training will retain some, if not all, of their pre-existing networks of support, making it easier for needs to be addressed as they arise, without their needing to be revealed in the training arena at all. This may be entirely appropriate. On the other hand, a balanced, non-residential training will also make space to deal with matters of formation and personal growth, and the freedom (or not) with which students and staff may express their personal concerns will depend, in part, on the emphasis given to that aspect of ministerial development. It would be easy to suggest that 'part-time' training can only offer 'part-time' ministerial formation. In practice, however, many non-residential courses seem to take this element more seriously, and are better at developing the 'whole person' than are their residential counterparts.[21]

Jesus' disciples neither went away to college, nor did they study part-time whilst continuing in their previous careers. Rather they 'left everything and followed him' (Luke 5:11). Their training was more like a full-time apprenticeship than a period of preparation in which they were set apart to equip them for their future ministries. They learned by being alongside Jesus, watching, listening and being involved as he directed. Sometimes they were successful; sometimes they made a mess of things. Always they looked to Jesus as their model. They were able to discuss things with him in private, to reflect on what had happened, ask for explanations and express surprise and incomprehension at what he said, without fear that he would give up on them.

The disciples' experience was unique. Yet it offers us a model of training which has all but disappeared in the Church of England,[22] although it continues to form a more significant part of training for other denominations (e.g. one year of four years' training for URC ministers). Three factors are crucial: firstly, the relationship with the person training is vital to the success of the exercise; secondly, knowledge and practice combine in 'hands-on' experience which can be reflected upon almost immediately; thirdly, failure is dealt with when it occurs and can be turned into an opportunity for personal and ministerial growth. Lastly, it all takes place in a context of worship, prayer and community which offers security to trainer and trainee alike.

From an Anglican point of view, it can be argued that the curacy period should equate to this apprenticeship model of training. In practice, the first three years of active ministry often feel a world apart from the period of initial (academic and skills) training. Few training incumbents are equipped to offer, or even have the time to encourage, effective reflection on the experiences of ministry, and many do not pray with their curates. The first curacy tends, therefore, to be an extension of the 'skills' element of initial training, and valuable as that is, ministerial formation is again a hidden item on the training agenda. There are, of course, exceptions, but many curates will receive little assistance in integrating knowledge, skills, reflection and prayer once they are ordained. Post-ordination training occasionally attempts to do this, but for many, it is 'too little, too late'.

In many ways the apprenticeship model would seem to be the most likely context in which a trainee minister might learn vulnerability, and undergo a period of effective ministerial formation. It is, perhaps, surprising, therefore, that there has been little impetus either to move in this direction for the period of *initial* training,[23] or to provide a structure of Continuing Ministerial Education (should it be called Continuing Ministerial *Formation*?) which allows for substantial periods of reflection and re-integration of knowledge, practice, prayer and personal development (for example, a period of three months at the end of a curacy or first incumbency?). Whilst the effectiveness of this approach depends, ultimately, on the trainer/ trainee relationship, potentially it has much to commend it in respect of ministerial formation.

Learning Vulnerability: the foundation

Prayer often feels like the 'also-ran' in training for ministry. It goes without saying that those who have been called to be leaders within the Christian community will be people of prayer; yet, sadly, 'it goes without saying' is often all too true. It is assumed that prayer happens both in the public context of communal worship and small group fellowship and in the personal devotions of each trainee minister. Help with prayer is available if required, but mostly, it is not talked about. It is spoken of as a subject in spirituality lectures and occasionally it is given chance and space to find its roots in a Quiet Day or

Retreat. In general, however, prayer is not on the ministerial agenda and is certainly not integrated into the academic, technical and reflective disciplines of ministerial training.

If prayer is at the heart of the way of vulnerability (see Chapter 3), then it is also at the heart of ministerial formation. Indeed, it is the foundation for learning vulnerability in a context of relationship. When either foundation or context are missing, or inadequate, then those who are trainee ministers are unlikely to choose to be vulnerable, so, perhaps, inhibiting their own and others' growth in ministry. Trainee ministers need to be actively supported in developing patterns of prayer which nurture their personal growth as they wrestle with the academic and pastoral demands of training. It is not simply a case of letting people get on with it; reflection on knowledge and practice must lead into and conjoin with the spiritual journey, rather than become yet another paper exercise. Reflection which is not re-integrated, in prayer as well as practice, is severely limited in its effect.

Learning vulnerability is, we would suggest, part of ministerial formation. In a training environment where the reality (if not the principle) of ministerial formation as integral to preparation for leadership in the Christian community has been or is in danger of being lost, those who are willing to risk walking the way of vulnerability may save the Church from success-bound professionalism, and ensure that the self-emptying, self-giving – sometimes vulnerable – service of others which *Christ* modelled, is not entirely effaced.

> *[Theological Colleges] have to become centers where people are trained in true discernment of the signs of the time. This cannot be just an intellectual training. It requires a deep spiritual formation involving the whole person – body, mind and heart. . . Everything in our competitive and ambitious world militates against it. But to the degree that such formation is being sought for and realized, there is hope for the Church of the next century.*[24]

NOTES

1. This chapter focuses particularly on training in the context of the Church of England.
2. Henri Nouwen, *In the Name of Jesus: Reflections on Christian Leadership* (London, DLT, 1989).
3. M. Basil Pennington, *Thomas Merton, Brother Monk* (San Francisco, Harper & Row, 1990), p. 156.
4. Kenneth Leech, *Spirituality and Pastoral Care* (London, Sheldon Press, 1986), p. 5.
5. ibid., p. 6.
6. General Synod of the Church of England, *Theological Training: A Way Ahead. A Report to the House of Bishops* (GS MISC 401), October 1992, p. 10.
7. ibid., p. 58.
8. Robert Borger and A. E. M. Seaborne, *The Psychology of Learning* (Harmondsworth, Middlesex, Penguin, 1966), p. 14.
9. Interestingly, John Perry in *Christian Leadership* (London, Hodder & Stoughton, 1983) sees vulnerability as an integral aspect of that learning:

    The leader who masks his vulnerability, perhaps out of fear caused by past hurts or rejection, can become remote and unreachable. When we are prepared to be vulnerable and open to others, we are saying that we want to go on learning in the school of leadership. This school lasts a lifetime. (p. 56)

10. Leech, p. 79.
11. P. Allan *et al.*, *The Fire and the Clay. The Priest in Today's Church* (London, SPCK, 1993).
12. See Chapter 5 on the nature of *conferred* and *derived* authority (p. 52). See also Chapter 12 on discernment.
13. See the example at the beginning of Chapter 5.
14. Some training institutions offer an 'independent' member of staff, or spiritual director, who is *not* responsible for any assessment of the trainee minister but who is available, specifically, to encourage personal and spiritual growth. For many ordinands, such help is invaluable. See Chapter 12 on Leadership.
15. *Theological Training: A Way Ahead. A Report to the House of Bishops.* pp. 94–5.
16. ibid., p. 137.
17. See John 15:5.
18. Pennington, p. 109.
19. Interestingly, in Luke 22:35–6 Jesus instructs his follows to *take up* purse and sword: what matters is that they choose an *appropriate* vulnerability.
20. See Chapters 2 and 4 especially.
21. For example, see an extract from GS MISC 401 (ibid.) concerning the South-West Ministerial Training Course:

    The syllabus is structured around three key words: Being, Knowing and Doing. Candidates are helped to deepen their knowledge of the biblical/theological foundations of their faith, and to acquire appropriate ministerial skills. But above all, they will be encouraged to develop greater self-awareness and spiritual depth so that knowledge and ability are allied to appropriate attitudes and personal integrity. (p. 121)

22. Such experience is now limited to a maximum of a one-month full-time place-ment in a parish for those in full-time training, less for those in part-time training.

23. An exception to this is the establishment of the 'Peterborough Project', part of the EAMTC for theology graduates, where a small group of ordinands may combine extended placements with academic study and theological reflection, built around a community base (cf. the ideas presented in a paper by The Revd Canon Dr Joy Tetley, 'Initial Training for Ordained Ministry: A Possible Way Forward', Appendix Q in GS MISC 401).

24. Nouwen, pp. 69f.

12

Prophetic Vulnerability: Community, Leadership and Discernment

The new hospital chaplain had only been in post for a short while. Becoming ill came as a shock, but it was some time before the reality came home. She who had been ministering to others now, at times, found others ministering to her. Her whole world was turned upside-down. As she lay in the hospital ward it was the cleaner who came to hold her hand, who re-assured her. She thought at first that she needed to acknowledge that she could no longer minister there. Then she realised that her ministry lay, for now, in being powerless, not powerful, and that in the way she allowed others to minister to her, she might reflect Christ's own ministry of handing over to others in surrender to God.

In Chapter 4 we affirmed the centrality of community at the heart of the Trinity. This community of the Trinity is such that 'Between Father, Son and Spirit, there is nothing but listening, receiving and giving . . .'[1] In our opening pastoral encounter, there are many signs of this listening, receiving and giving – and the recognition that community may not be structured, but may be an informal and transient encounter between those who believe. It also indicates that within a community centred on God there are different kinds of leadership which are exercised, some of them formalised though not, by any means, all.[2]

In this chapter we attempt to define 'community' more precisely and to explore the role of the leader in enabling the community to discern God's will and 'own' its vision. As always our focus is on the person of Christ and lying behind much of this and the next chapter is the account in John 13 of Jesus washing the disciples' feet.

Community

Perhaps some of the greatest tensions which arise in a community of any kind derive, fundamentally, from the fact that individual members have very different expectations and assumptions about the nature of the community to which they belong.

> *A meeting of the village council was getting nowhere. The farmers argued that the land should not be used for housing; the village school's teacher knew that unless more children were to come into the village, the school would close; the publican knew he needed more customers. The Chairman of the Council, a relative newcomer to the village, wanted only to maintain the 'traditional' character of the village – the image of the village which had originally attracted him to make it his home.*

The examples are numerous – people have different images of what a community is. If progress is to be made, many of those images – illusions – will be smashed, as people recognise that a community is necessarily a complex web of different hopes and aspirations. The term 'community' itself is usually only a partial way of describing the reality.

Some . . . seem to overstate the degree to which the Church can be viewed as a community, given that the Church is most often a network or networks which crystallise at certain points in public worship or action.[3]

If we turn from the more general use of the word to the concept of one particular Christian community, we find that there too people have different images. Bonhoeffer writes:

The serious Christian, set down for the first time in a Christian community, is likely to bring with him a very definite idea of what Christian life together should be and try to realise it. But God's grace speedily shatters such dreams.[4]

And he argues that only when those dreams are shattered do we truly encounter the reality of God, others and ourselves.

In other words there is no such thing as a perfect Christian community. The disciples, having been so long with Jesus, must have been shattered that one of their number would receive the bread and then go out into the night to betray Jesus (John 13:30).

We are broken persons and live in broken communities in a state of brokenness. We are alienated from ourselves and from each other. We do not readily fit together. We are like a bunch of porcupines trying to huddle together for warmth who are always driven apart out of fear for the wounds we can inflict on each other with our quills.[5]

Indeed, community can be a fearful place of isolation, but it also has the potential to be a 'safe' place of nurture and growth. It is this latter kind of community that may help us most truly reflect the life of the Trinity. To develop such a community means that we actually accept 'finitude' – not only our own but that of others, not only that of individuals but also the imperfections of human communities themselves. Acceptance of 'finitude' suggests immediately that we need God's grace if community is to flourish. For true community is a gift: we are one, we share fellowship in the biblical sense only because we are in Christ (Gal. 3:28), embraced by the community of the Trinity, loved and blessed.[6]

Christianity means community through Jesus Christ and in Jesus Christ. No Christian community is more or less than this. Whether it be a brief, single encounter or the daily fellowship of years, Christian community is only this. We belong to one another only through and in Jesus Christ.[7]

It is because we are already in this fundamental community that 'those points of crystallisation' and incidental encounters in life, as in our first example in this chapter, can become times of revelation of the presence of Christ. The joy of Christian life is that we 'touch' on *this* community in a way which often crosses boundaries at many levels so, while the denominations debate doctrine, people of prayer know this essential unity.

There is however a need to define what we mean by Christian community in the practical sense of setting those boundaries which enable the 'porcupines' to live together more equably. John English makes the useful distinction between any Christian group and a Christian community. The latter 'is found in the sense of self-identity shared by the members, that is, their interior sense of unity and responsibility. The sense of unity is the special unity of covenant.'[8] If we are to engage in a community where vulnerability is possible and used *appropriately* for individual and corporate affirmation, healing and growth, a clear understanding of community is necessary if inappropriate vulnerability is to be avoided. Many groupings of Christians are not specifically community except in the wider, though deep, sense of being 'in Christ'. Unless there is a covenant (however informally made) between the people involved in the group, it may still be subject to many and varied expectations. When a group agrees on its identity, its calling by God, and members commit themselves to loving loyally, however, they experience Christ in a different way by providing a *covenanted* love for each other. Depending on the purpose of such a group, it is likely that here will be a 'safe' place.

In Chapter 4 we noted the need of such a 'safe' place if masks are to be removed and people are to find a place for self-revelation and vulnerability. Thus within any understanding of Christian community, we might expect to see a reflection of the forgiveness, reconciliation and love which lie at the heart of God – an image of porcupines, who have the potential and the means of grace to make peace.

A community whose members so covenant with each other, to 'be there for each other', may be no more then than a few people who meet regularly to share their stories, to support each other in their vocation and prayers. Alternatively, a community may require structure and organisation if it is to fulfil its mission. Such structure will at times be deeply resented by some, but without it the community would be like a body without a skeleton.[9] Indeed, as we have already observed, a community without clear guidelines as to its purpose and mission may be making itself vulnerable in ways which are inappropriate – leaving itself open to division and intense wrangling, thus depleting energy and stifling the Spirit.

In seeking to foster a healthy community where vulnerability has a place, it soon becomes clear that there needs to be both 'enclosure' (the equivalent of an individual's need for solitude) and 'encounter' with others and with the wider world (something we shall explore further in Chapter 13).

Leadership

The image of Jesus bending down to wash the disciples' feet in John 13 is, in 'prophetic action', a reflection of Jesus' words in Luke 10:45: 'for the Son of Man came not to be served but to serve, and to give his life as a ransom for many'. For Christ, and so for us, the way of leadership is the way of service.

The Leader is to serve the community and enable the community, both individually and corporately, to become more truly that which God would have.

the community belongs to the community. Its sanctity and success do not rise and fall on the shoulders of one leader alone. They rise and fall on the shoulders of its members. What they are the community shall be.[10]

In a sense, within the Christian community, all are leaders – all have the possibility of being Christ for one another; but if a community is to have structure, it is necessary for the community's freedom that some people be given authority over certain areas of its life. The bearing of this authority may be costly. The Taizé Rule, for example, reminds us that the person who bears authority 'more than anyone else . . . needs your support and mercy'.[11]

In showing a Leader 'support and mercy', we may question how far we should mark out such a Leader from the rest of the community. Such separation, emphasised, for example, by freehold and tied housing can bring enormous pressures. Clergy families living in tied accommodation can experience undue stress which may result in marital breakdown and unreasonable expectations that the clergy home will be 'open house'. The vulnerability experienced by clergy families also needs to be, as far as possible, a *chosen* one rather than one inflicted by the system!

The Leader too will have issues to address in his or her own journey for, like the community, no Leader is perfect.

The man who commands you is a sinner and you, still imperfect, obey. Yet through this twofold expression of the imperfection of master and disciple you will be led into the way of perfection, where you will never lack grace as long as you are trustful, open and persevering.[12]

To lead a community brings not only vulnerability but also loneliness. Often such Leaders carry knowledge relating to individuals which they must hold within themselves, and in their prayer. They may, in being true to the community's vocation and charism, need to challenge members of the community. They may, in holding fast to community decisions, have to disappoint the desires of an individual. Leaders need then, for their own sake, to model themselves on Christ so that they are alone 'yet not alone' (John 16:32), for in the person of Christ, the Father is with them.

There is also the loneliness of decision-making. Although most decisions may be made by the community or by authorised groups within it, there are always decisions which on a day-to-day basis call for wisdom and discernment for the Leader alone. Leaders live with risk. The Leader may also at times be very aware of the need to wear 'masks'[13] in order to be totally 'there' for members of the community.

If such loneliness is to be borne, it is important that the Leader find some form of 'accompaniment' which may well need to come from outside the community. Jean Vanier points to different kinds of accompaniment that all members of a community may need[14] – a companion on the spiritual journey, a companion in the work situation, a companion in community life and, for some, the professional companionship of a psychologist or other therapist. For the Leaders, such companions from outside the community provide much loving support and help them maintain their own journey and vision. In this way they support not only the Leader but the whole community.

Discernment

We have already described in Chapter 7 how discernment took place in a particular situation (see pp. 78–9). We now need to explore the role of discernment in community life and the levels of consultation and involvement that may be helpful.

A theological college, several years ago, based itself on a monastic model. The students, all male and single, lived in community, worshipped, ate and worked together. To define such a community and who should be involved in the process of discernment was relatively simple. A theological college now may be made up of women and men, married and single students. There may now be many children too. Some married students may commute daily or at weekends. To define 'community' may be more difficult. Indeed in discernment and decision-making it may be necessary to identify several 'layers' of community. It may also be important to decide which constituency should make particular decisions and also to decide which constituency should be consulted.

Clarity on such issues can ensure that such a community is enabled to live with differences in constructive ways.

It also helps to be clear in what areas the leader is empowered to make decisions and where other decisions are to be made, whether by the whole community or an elected group within it. Only then may we expect 'obedience' to be a part of community life. 'To "obey", from the Latin *ab audire*, to hear or listen to, is to submit freely to the word that has been heard because its truth has been guaranteed by God who is Truth itself.'[15] To obey is to listen attentively, and for the Hebrew mind to listen attentively is to listen with the whole of one's being and then, hearing God, to obey naturally and without hesitation. There was no separate word for 'obey'. Within a 'covenanted' community such listening and obedience may take many forms. Certainly individuals' own listening to God in prayer lies at the heart of all other obedience, but if the community is to be truly a community, obedience must be not only the individual obeying his own discernment of God's call but also contributing to the discernment of the community and 'obeying' that discernment even when, individually, he may have chosen differently.

In Chapter 5 we made the distinction between conferred and derived authority. What we are now arguing for is a true obedience to 'conferred authority'.

We have to learn how to obey people who have been appointed or elected to responsibility according to the constitution, even if we do not feel any great friendship or affection for them. . . It is not necessary to have total trust in the individuals with authority. But we should trust the people who have elected them . . . and the system.[16]

Discernment by the community is no more than a natural progression of 'obedience'. Spiritual discernment, in the context of this present book, may best be described as seeking to listen to the guidance of the Holy Spirit in order to follow the Spirit's lead into the person of Christ, and thereby into the heart of the Trinity and into the mission of the Holy Trinity to embrace the world.

Discernment is a skill which is gained and nurtured by practice. John English identifies five stages:[17]

1. Experience.
2. Reflection on a period of life.
3. Articulation: to express what is happening from a Christian perspective, maybe to another person, within a small group or through keeping a journal.
4. Interpretation: the recognition of the significance of the movement of spirits that have been discovered through reflection and experience.
5. Decision and action: 'obedience' to what one trusts the Spirit is drawing one to do.

This process may be an individual one or one undertaken by a group or community.[18] Once the drawing of the Spirit has been discerned, it is helpful to ask the Lord for some kind of 'confirmation' of the proposed plan of action. Such confirmation may be, for example, a common sense of well-being even though the decision involves much cost and hardship. It is enough to know that the community is being drawn into closer fellowship with Christ, even if that fellowship is in 'sharing his sufferings' (1 Cor. 1:9; Phil. 3:10).

Clearly the Leader may play a key role in enabling this task of discernment, both encouraging a community to engage in it and in resisting too hasty decisions, in waiting for confirmation.

A church extension project was abandoned, and a new project had to be devised. The church council (who had the 'legal' standing

and responsibility to make decisions and was thereafter liable)
agreed a pattern of meetings to make decisions. Church meetings
were held to consult with members of the entire congregation. A
meeting with neighbours was held to consult the local 'community'.
The PCC appointed an executive to advise the PCC and to make
day-to-day decisions but set a financial limit above which those
decisions had to be referred to the PCC. A new project was even-
tually agreed which, within the church, had almost unanimous
support despite the cost and the practical implications. The whole
process was enfolded by prayer.

This example draws out some of the practical implications of discernment and emphasises the need for clear lines of accountability and
authority as well as the need to build 'consultation' and the taking
of advice from within and outside the community into decision-
making.

Truth

Jesus promises us a Spirit which will lead us into all truth (John
8:32). Discernment, if it is listening to that Spirit, is really based on
being familiar with Christ, coming to recognise his ways – his gentleness, attractiveness drawing us to life. It takes time to practise it and
it is an on-going process:

We must put our confidence in truth. But that doesn't mean sitting back and
waiting for the truth to shine from above, as one might sit back and wait for
the day to break. It means following with devoted obedience the truth we
have seen as true with an entire confidence in God, that he will correct, clear
and redirect our vision, to the perception of a freer and deeper truth. Go with
the truth you have and let it carry you into collision with the hard rocks of
fact and then you'll learn something.[19]

In reality, listening means becoming informed of facts: of the tradition
of the Church, of the particular circumstances about which the
decision is to be made, about the people involved. There are no short
cuts. Prayer on its own is illusory. It is holding prayer and reality
together which will guide us towards a clearer way. In promising the

freedom that the Spirit of truth will bring, Jesus also reminds us that we need to abide in his words – be 'pickled' in scripture and live it authentically.[20] Even when we then come to a decision, discernment continues; as we live our partial truth with integrity we stay watchful as a clearer truth may emerge. For example, the financial straits of the Church of England in the 1980s are often seen only in a negative light. Is it not conceivable that through them the Spirit has enabled the Church to develop, by necessity, a more collaborative ministry? What appeared as crisis may be considered in future generations a remarkable gift.

In looking at Community, Leadership and the task of Discernment, we have recognised that 'now we see in a mirror dimly'. We have seen discernment in a comprehensive way: listening to how the Spirit is moving in the community, how the Spirit has led in the past, and listening to the Spirit's breath through Scripture and prayer, as well as looking at reality so that we may be led into greater truth. Community, leadership and discernment are seldom perfect tools of God's Kingdom, but they are the tools to hand. All we can do is keep practising!

First, as a doctor practises medicine, the Church practises community, following the example of Jesus. Second, the sinful and divided Church has only the capacity to practise – it is far from achieving perfection. Third, this practice is not to create an insular community but rather to demonstrate and evoke – however partially – the practice of community in all the networks of society.[21]

NOTES

1. Pierre-Marie Delfieux, *A City Not Forsaken: The Rule of the Jerusalem Community* (London, DLT, 1985), p. 67.
2. For the sake of clarity, in the next two chapters we will use 'Leader' to refer primarily to the person with overall conferred authority of a community and 'leader' to refer to those who share that leadership. Often, but not always, what is said of the Leader may apply too to the leaders.
3. *ABM Ministry paper, no 1* (London, ABM, 1991), p. 10.
4. Dietrich Bonhoeffer, *Life Together* (London, SCM Press, 1954), p. 15.

5. M. Basil Pennington, *Thomas Merton, Brother Monk* (San Francisco, Harper & Row, 1990), p. 125.

6. See Chapter 9 (p. 90).

7. Bonhoeffer, p. 10.

8. John English, *Spiritual Intimacy and Community* (London, DLT, 1992), p. 16.

9. We are much indebted to Jean Vanier's *Community and Growth* (London, DLT, 1989) in this chapter. The image of the skeleton is on p. 9.

10. Joan Chittister, *The Rule of Benedict* (UK, St Pauls, 1992), p. 91.

11. Henri Nouwen, *Rule For a New Brother* (London, DLT, 1973), p. 15.

12. Delfieux, p. 67.

13. See Chapter 4 above.

14. See especially Vanier, pp. 249–51.

15. *Catechism of the Catholic Church* (London, Geoffrey Chapman, 1994), para. 144.

16. Vanier, p. 231. For the Church of England as an established church, this must surely raise questions about the role of the Prime Minister and the appointment of Bishops. Speaking of this issue, Dr Christina Baxter writes 'secrecy breeds mistrust of the system . . . this mitigates against one of the three main aims of the Church of England in this quinquennium – to increase confidence amongst its members' in *The Church of England Year Book 1998* (London, Church House Publishing, 1998), p. xxvii.

17. English, pp. 29ff.

18. ibid. is immensely helpful in this area.

19. Austin Farrer, *The End of Man* (London, SPCK, 1973).

20. See 'Pickled in the Word' in Chapter 14 (pp. 169f).

21. Robin Greenwood, *Practising Community* (London, SPCK, 1996), p. 1.

13

Prophetic Vulnerability:
Leader and Community Together

... by removing his garments Jesus is revealing his true glory, his deepest self, his heart's most intimate desire. He becomes smaller and smaller, more and more vulnerable in order to communicate love. Often we admire people who are important, but we are also a bit frightened of them. We are drawn to love someone who seems little and who needs us. That is where the mystery of Jesus lies: he becomes smaller and humble in order to live with the disciples the same union and communion he lives with his Father... To wash the feet of a brother or sister in Christ, to allow someone to wash our feet, is a sign that together we want to follow Jesus, to take the downward path, to find Jesus' presence in the poor and the weak. Is it not a sign that we too want to live a heart-to-heart relationship with others, to meet them as a person and a friend and to live in communion with them? Is it not a sign also that we yearn to be men and women of forgiveness, to be healed and cleansed and to heal and cleanse others and thus to live more fully in communion with Jesus?[1]

The image that St John gives us in John 13 is of Jesus at one with his disciples. It is a meal of the chosen ones, a meal in which love will set Peter free into a deeper intimacy and will set Judas free to go out into the night. The opportunity is being given of greater communion with Jesus. Times such as these are times when not only individuals but also the community is drawn into a deeper and more honest fellowship.

In Chapter 12 we observed that a community will always need

times of *enclosure* and of *encounter*. Here, we develop those ideas, relating them to the Church's nature as being one, holy, catholic and apostolic. In the light of this, we also look at the nature of priesthood and its relationship with the wider community.

Enclosure and Encounter

I try to enter the vision of God, in his triune life, looking upon his world: men and women, aimless, despairing, hateful and killing, men and women sick and dying, the old and the young, the rich and the poor, the happy and the sad, some being born and some laid to rest. The leap of divine joy: God knows that the time has come when the mystery of his salvific plan, hidden from the beginning of the world will be made manifest.[2]

Our calling is to enter the life of the Trinity, a life which speaks of deep relationship and intimacy, both within the Being of God and with the world to which he has made himself vulnerable. The former aspect concerns the relationships which we have with each other and our own self-identity that we reflect in 'enclosure'; the latter, that vulnerability to the world which we reflect in 'encounter'.

As we ponder John 13–16 we see Christ encouraging his disciples in a mutual, loyal love to be revealed in service – to maintain 'enclosure'; yet he also prepares them for the 'encounter' with a hostile world. They will need a loving intimacy with each other and with him, but they will also need the vision not to be limited by such intimacy. If they are to bear fruit, they will need to be ready for pruning as well as harvest. Only then will their joy be complete (John 15).

The Church is 'One'[3]

To maintain the unity of a community we need to heighten our awareness of our unity in Christ[4] and its day-to-day implications in other relationships.

> *A group sat in a circle around a single candle. They were asked to look at the person opposite them. Looking through the candle's*

*light, the light of Christ, they could see clearly the face of the
person. Then they were asked to look away from the candle and
look at the person next to them. As they looked they saw that
much of the face was in shadow . . . and then they realised – so
was theirs.*

It is when we know ourselves and others 'in the person of Christ' that
we find the unity we seek and the grace necessary to be committed to
each other and to a life of truth and reconciliation.

Community is not about perfect people. It is about people who are bonded
to each other, each of whom is a mixture of good and bad, darkness and
light, love and hate. . . There is a part of us which is already luminous, already
converted. And there is a part of us which is still in shadow. A community is
not made up only of the converted. It is made up of all the elements in us
which need to be transformed, purified and pruned. It is made up also of the
unconverted.[5]

The unity of the community depends, therefore, on a constant work
of reconciliation: facing tensions in God's time, learning the art of
forgiveness and being a place of healing love.[6]

What then is the Leader's role?

If Jesus is to minister to his people, then Leaders must be, as far
as it lies with them, transparent to his love, allowing all that they are
to be accessible to him so that, through them, he may love his
disciples. Their task is to be a 'John the Baptist' figure always pointing
others to Christ and away from themselves.[7] St Benedict's Rule says
simply: 'Let them prefer nothing whatever to Christ'.[8] In so pointing
people to Christ – always showing them respect and love – the Leader
may encourage five things: to love the Church – the Body of Christ;
to bear the tradition – the presence of Christ through the ages; to be
engaged in partnership; to be ready to wash feet; and to offer pastoral
care.

Love the Church

The Leader is not commissioned to exercise an individualistic ministry but to play a part in the ministry of the whole Church. It is,
perhaps, easier to believe in an individual as a loved sinner than to

believe in an institution, patently imperfect, yet loved by God. Yet, failure to love God's people – even in the corporate guise of the Church – is failure to love Christ (Matt. 25 and John 13:34). The unity of the local community necessarily involves a sometimes critical unity with the wider Church. The Leader of a community, by reflecting the vision of that community to the wider fellowship of the Church and also reflecting the wider visions of the universal Church to the community, nurtures a sometimes fragile unity.

Bearer of Tradition

In the practice of Spiritual Direction the 'Director's' task is to listen to another person's story and to listen for the 'whistle of the gentle air' of the Spirit, giving direction to their relationship with God. Similarly, the Leader may listen to the Spirit's leading in the life of the Church, local and universal, in order to keep the community aware of how the Spirit has brought them thus far and also where he might be leading (Jer. 6:16, Isa. 30:21). In this way, tradition becomes not a burden but the joy of recognising Christ at work in his Church through the ages.

In Partnership

Partnership is Jesus' call to Peter in John 13 – a privilege echoed in John 21 with the call to tend the flock. 'Unless I wash you, you have no *share* with me.' We are to share in his life, in his suffering and resurrection, and in his ministry – to be co-workers with him, and co-workers with each other. The Leader needs to be in partnership with his community and working alongside others, recognising, promoting and encouraging others in their vocation. Speaking of the ordained ministry Robin Greenwood suggests

on the one hand the Church needs ordained ministers to remind the community of the divine mission in which they are engaged and the grace of God on which they are dependent and by which they are built up. On the other hand, ordained ministry has no proper existence apart from, in one way or another, the local church community.[9]

Ready to Wash Feet

In following Christ, the Leader is called to serve and respect the 'flock' he tends. Bonhoeffer argues that a Leader should never lose respect for a community for 'a congregation has not been entrusted to him in order that he should become its accuser before God'.[10] The cost of love is high and loss of respect for those in our care an ill-afforded luxury. It is daunting to imagine Jesus washing Judas' feet, but also necessary.

Pastoral Care

If the Leader is to play his part in maintaining the unity of the community, he will need to be aware of relationships within the community and where there are areas of vulnerability in relationships. The greater task is to discern where the vulnerability is appropriate and where it is not, and then discerning a course of action. He will also care for individuals. Bonhoeffer reminds us, 'He who loves community, destroys community: he who loves the brethren builds community.'[11]

Again we may say that it is not just the Leader but all who exercise leadership who may share in this task of encouraging all members of a community to maintain its unity: the task of pointing to Christ, of listening for the Spirit's song in the resonances of people's lives and relationships, of loving without exception and of daring to forgive and be forgiven. In such ways may we reveal to others Jesus' deep respect and the divine courtesy.

The Church is 'catholic'

A Christ-centred community is

a living community in which the Spirit of the risen Christ has free play. Through the varied distance of his charism the Spirit enables men in such a community to grow truly human through deep relationships with God and with their fellow human beings. Within this rich variety of gifts – charisms of service that make for growth, unity and fullness of life – is the charism of authority, which is always presented in the New Testament as a special and important form of service.[12]

Although the author is speaking of a monastic community, he reiterates for us the need in any Christian community for all to take responsibility for the spiritual gifts with which they are entrusted. He also recognises the gift of authority. The pattern is of collaborative ministry where all serve each other as they have been served by Christ – but also of a community which is not cynical or antagonistic of authority. 'Each individual person in the community must be nourished in love. If not he or she will ... be in opposition to the community.'[13]

This love of each other needs discernment too. It is possible for a small number, even a single individual who is deeply wounded, to seek more and more attention. Love on its own may not be enough. People may need professional accompaniment if they are to come to wholeness. The love that Christ reveals draws people not to ever greater dependence but to grow to their full stature, to become 'more tomorrow than they were today'.[14] For this to happen it may be necessary that the community stay alongside in love whilst others, more professionally trained and with relevant personal gifts, are used for healing.[15] The alternative is sometimes the offering of a false love which fails to address the reality of the deep woundedness which cries out for healing. Love itself will sometimes be the way in which these wounds, long hidden, may be revealed:

love makes us weak and vulnerable because it breaks down the barriers and protective armour we have built around ourselves. Love means letting others reach us and being sensitive enough to reach them. The cement of unity is interdependence ... community is made by the gentle concern that people show each other every day.[16]

The role of the leader in such a community is to love in realistic, sustainable ways, 'to the end', and to encourage others in that loving. Such love needs to be both spontaneous and – through reflection and discernment – self-aware. We need both to be aware of the effect we have on others, and vigilant about maintaining their independence. It is important that the Leader does not assume sole responsibility but engages others in the pastoral task and in the discernment process when individual vocations are being pursued. In all of this there is a specific need to ensure confidentiality, to avoid making others vulnerable in an inappropriate way. Boundaries need to be recognised even if, as discussed in Chapter 10, we sometimes knowingly cross them, and it is vital for the whole community that the Leader keep the good of the whole in mind when dealing with individuals.

The Church is 'apostolic'

I am convinced communal life can flourish only if it exists for an aim outside itself. Community is viable if it is the outgrowth of a deep involvement in a purpose which is other than, or above, that of becoming a community.[17]

To listen to the Spirit's song at the Last Supper is to hear Jesus say 'This is my body given for you', 'This is my blood, shed for you and for many for the forgiveness of sins.' The kenosis of Christ is his being poured out for 'the many', οι πολλοι ('hoi polloi') as well as for the sake of the disciples. In him, we too are to be poured out for the one and the many. We are, in essence, neither more nor less than the blood of Christ poured out for the world, the bread which must be 'taken, blessed, broken and shared that the work of the incarnation may go forward'.[18]

It is not possible to eat the broken body of Christ in the Eucharist and to drink his blood shed for us through torture, and not open our hearts to the broken and crucified people in our world today.[19]

This opening of hearts in encounter is the responsibility of the whole community and needs, as all else, careful discernment, and an agreed approach. Often a community's mission will relate to its original vocation, though time and circumstance may shape ever new approaches to its fulfilment.

Leadership in such a community involves encouraging its mission in five ways: by reflection on its mission and a commitment to prayer; by living the gospel; by being true to the discernment process through faithful listening; by being true to its mission and by being true to itself.

Reflection

The preaching and teaching responsibility . . . is to make a contribution to the reflective discipleship of the laity, rather than to teach *all* that is needed or do their thinking for them. Clergy and Laity are learning together.[20]

As Daniel Rees *et al.* say of the abbot in a Benedictine community, the Leader is to be 'an educative guide in the life of the Spirit', to teach as much by how they live as by what they say. The Leader,

more than anyone else needs to listen to what the Spirit is saying to the Churches: what he is saying to this little flock within the universal church, and what he is saying *today*, not merely what he was saying yesterday.[21]

The Leader then must have time to read, pray and reflect – alone and with others. If it is Christ's leadership and vulnerability we desire to follow, then we need to identify with him by going with him to a lonely place (John 6:14),[22] to enter his solitude and prayer. Similarly, part of the role of those who teach and preach is to help people identify *their* story with Jesus' story, *their* life with his life – both individually and corporately – and in Chapter 14 we shall see how that identification is carried forward in and through the worship of the community. This identification with Christ takes us to the deepest levels of unity and to deeper understanding of our identity and mission.

Living the Gospel

It was said of Jesus that 'they were astounded at his teaching because he spoke as one with authority' (Luke 4:32).

It is the disciplined offering of themselves and the receiving of grace which gives ministers the inner authority which people recognise. It is as they live the Gospel which they proclaim that they commend it to others. If something of Christ is reflected in them and found to be attractive others will then be open to listen to what they have to say.[23]

In other words, clergy must live not only out of their *conferred* authority but also the deep, *derived* authority that comes from prayer, reflection on experience, authentic living and theological insight.[24]

Faithful Listening
Perhaps the greatest threat to visible unity is when a community undergoes periods of great change, times when the shared vision may not be clear and where struggle predominates. In such times, just as Christ did for his disciples, the Leader will recall the community to the love which lies at the heart of all, and will seek to encourage a deep listening to each other and to God. Encouraging a community to wait for clear discernment is not an easy task, but is often a necessary part of the vulnerability that a community and its leaders must share as they seek to follow Christ's way.

True to its Mission
Often the role of leader is to gently draw the community back to its agreed mission. If the community has prayerfully discerned its vision and received confirmation of that task, then it will need to be constantly reminded of its calling. There will always be other demands on the community's resources. The Leader, though, will wisely and gently keep the vision alive, not only in the way it is communicated, but also in the way he or she lives that vision out.

True to Itself
A leader is more of a clown than a ring master. It is the clown who shows us the way of vulnerability, who makes himself available to people and who is prepared to risk being outrageous for the sake of others. We need to discover 'our own unique fullness' and to discover our own unique style of leadership which allows God free access to use our whole range of frailties and gifts. Jack Dominian writes:

Fullness and wholeness means that a person has as much access to himself as possible and that the various components are at balance with each other. I refer to this as the integrity of the person. It is out of such integrity that authentic behaviour emanates. The word 'authentic' is derived from the Greek and means literally, 'One who does a thing himself' . . . What the person does derives its validity because it comes from the integrity of the self. It no longer depends on the presence of fear, the need to please, to placate, to do something for another which does not correspond to the genuine intention of the doer. . .[25]

The Church is 'holy'

The call to priesthood, as any vocation, is (amongst others) a call to holiness, to intimate relationship, to affirmation of identity, and to partnership in the divine mission.

. . . the ordained ministry has a different purpose and responsibility from that of the laity. This involves ordained ministries in contributing to all other ministries, by helping to form and clarify the latter in such a way that the other ministries can exemplify and sustain the four marks of the Church. The ordained ministry is to draw out the marks of the Church. . . The four marks of the Church, for which the ordained have specific though not sole responsibility, are as much to do with the encounter of the Church with the world as with the internal life and ordering of the Church.[26]

In so drawing out the marks of the Church, those who are ordained reflect, in a limited way, the nature of the Trinity, where:

The three persons of the Trinity in perichoretic relationship do not simply take up an attitude of loving concern towards each other, but actually make each other who they are through loving relation. Their separate, different contribution to the Trinitarian being and work is inseparable from the relationship between them.[27]

Holiness

In John 17 Jesus prays that as he sanctifies himself so his disciples will be sanctified. The Church is to be holy as Christ is holy. The task of the Church is to reveal that holiness in and through its worship – a major means of our corporate formation – and through its involvement in the Kingdom ministry:

The ordained ministry serves the holiness of the Church by pointing the Church to the holiness of Christ and by developing the holiness of Christ in the Church . . . the ordained need to foster habits of prayer and penitence, of self-criticism and self-awareness as those with a responsibility to participate in the holiness of Jesus Christ.[28]

In other words we are suggesting that the ordained ministry has a part to play in the spiritual formation of particular members of the community and in the corporate formation of the whole community. That task may be no more than just being attentive to the community. Jean Vanier writes:

When the Priest or minister has no power, other than that which comes from his ordination, he has enormous freedom to be truly present throughout the community, and in all aspects of community life, on equal terms with everyone. He is stranger to nobody and there is no situation beyond his touch – which must always be that of Jesus. He is free to meet everyone, to be anywhere and by his presence to be a living reminder of the place of Jesus and the gospels in the community. It is simply by being present among his people that the priest will come to know their joys and anxieties and there he will find a thousand opportunities for shining the light of God on all that touches the lives of the members of the community.[29]

Intimate Relationships
We noted in Chapter 2 that

The 'condescending God' in the person of his incarnate Son, Jesus Christ, establishes a relationship of love between himself and humanity which is faithful and true and ultimately costly. That costly vulnerability was made possible only because of the security of the relationships – with God and with his closest followers – in which he was set. Vulnerability is only possible in such a context.

The priest is called to a deepening relationship with God and relationships of trust with fellow workers.

Identity
We have already said that in living out their calling priests do not lose their self-identity. Rather it is the opposite: if the vocation is real, responding to it confirms identity and is a 'coming home' to self. The image of Christ's baptism is the relevant 'ikon' of vocation. In his baptism (John 1:32–4 and parallels) Jesus is affirmed by John

and by the heavenly voice. It is true to our experience too that we are affirmed when those who test our vocation confirm our sense of calling. In all ministry we need human as well as divine affirmation, the converging of inner and outer voices.

Partnership

The call of ministry is not only to follow Christ but to work with him in partnership, and in partnership with all others who minister in his name. It is in this partnership that we most truly reflect the life of the Trinity.

Priesthood and Leadership

How then may this be made real? Why and how are clergy given authority? And what is the relationship between Clergy and Laity?

Authority

In the same way that our holiness derives from the holiness of Christ so the priesthood of all believers derives from the priesthood of Christ. The ordained ministry is then a ministry which gains its authority from the priesthood of all believers.

the ordained ministry serves the interests of the Church so that through ordination the Church, amongst other things, *confers* an *authority* and *representativeness* upon those who are ordained. The Church recognises ordination as the public identifying of those who *carry particular responsibility, under authority* and *with accountability.* (our italics)[30]

In the same way that there may be transient and informal experiences of 'community', there may be periods when leadership is exercised by different members of a community and in many different ways. What makes the ordained ministry different is that their vocation has been tested and tried over a period of time; it has been recognised and affirmed both informally and through selection procedures, and they have then undergone a period of intensive training before being given authority to minister. If vulnerability is being embraced, the importance of being under authority and accountable to others is underlined. We would argue, as we did in

Chapter 10, that the ordained ministry is not a 'profession' but rather a professional ministry. As such, the realisation of being under authority and the clarity of accountability is more necessary than ever. This 'accompaniment'[31] in the work setting is one element of the necessary strands of accompaniment by which the ordained minister is supported. Being able to trust this support makes the 'space' in which they may be able to continue their own formation, for our formation 'in the person of Christ' is a life-long process. It is in such ways that local ministers are clearly recognised and supported in seeing their ministry as part of the work of the whole Church.

Clergy and Laity

Vocation to the ordained ministry is not a denial of the priesthood of all believers but actually confirms it. The priest is authorised by that wider priesthood and in some ways will be representative of it. If we are to understand the relationship between the clergy and laity, we need to return again to the Trinity. The members of the Trinity, though distinct, are – at the same time – in a dynamic dance of love which, rather than obliterate their distinctiveness, actually enhances it and affirms individual identity: so Jesus gazing at the Father loves the Father into a deeper knowledge of Fatherhood, and Jesus affirmed by the Father in his baptism and Transfiguration is deepened in his experience of sonship.[32]

At their best, clergy are to confirm the call of members of the laity in calling them to holiness, as discussed above, but also engaging in a relationship of warm positive regard – the gaze of love – in affirming identity and in working in partnership. In the relationship between clergy and laity each may encourage the other to be faithful to their unique calling. Clergy and laity are responsible for themselves and for one another, for it is in relationship and partnership that we follow Christ.

... persons exist only in relationship, a relationship in which there is necessarily interaction, mutual critique, mutual formation of the persons.[33]

In bringing these two chapters concerning community and leadership to a close we may draw out some key areas for further thought and reflection.

- Freehold and tied housing can bring enormous pressures. Perhaps it is time to review clergy salaries and conditions of service in order that clergy families may not become 'the victims' of inappropriate vulnerability.
- 'Holy Management' relies heavily on discernment: a listening to the Spirit in the inner life as well as a listening to the Spirit in the known facts of the situation and in the available sources of possible guidance – scripture, tradition and reason. Such discernment is ongoing.
- Collaborative ministry is built upon the differing gifts and temperaments of all God's people. It is when such gifts and temperaments are set free that we allow a full flow of energy for the Kingdom. When gifts are stifled and people employed in situations which go against their natural temperaments, much energy may be wasted. Other than Christ, there is no 'blueprint' of what a priest should be. Different people will exercise their priesthood in different ways within the ultimate calling to serve the Church, while remaining under the authority and accountability we have already stressed.
- Those in leadership in the Church need clear structures of support/ supervision and accountability, and we have underlined, too, the need for 'accompaniment' for those who minister in community.
- There will be times when a non-collaborative style of leadership may be necessary. The question is always 'What style is most appropriate to serving the people of God in this particular situation?'
- Those selected for training for ministry will have a fundamental task in 'acting as a theological and leadership resource'.[34] The need for training to be founded on spiritual formation cannot be overemphasised.
- Those trained for leadership, and especially those ordained, will need to be flexible in their ways of working. It is the task of those who appoint to prayerfully discern the needs of the post, the temperament as well as the qualifications needed, of the person needed and the suitability of applicants. At every level of ministry, the relevant community needs not only to be part of the discernment process but also needs to have trust in the 'system'.

- The leadership itself and the pastoral care of the community belongs to the community and is shared. 'The role of the ordained ministry is to serve and service the whole ministry of the people of God.'[35] We need to set these people free to fully use the gifts they have in order that they, in their turn, may be agents of liberation as they share in the ministries of the churches they serve, and as they encounter the wider world.
- The Spirit is calling churches to a ministry of reconciliation in a broken world. It is in this *togetherness* that priesthood assumes its most urgent vulnerability.
- 'Enclosure' is not a reason for failing to look or love outside community.
- 'Encounter' is not a reason for failing to love our brothers and sisters.

Will you agree to set out on this road? At the risk of losing your life
for love, will you
live Christ for others?[36]

Whose feet will you wash?[37]

NOTES

1. Jean Vanier, *The Scandal of Service* (London, DLT, 1997), pp. 49, 83.
2. David L. Fleming sj, *The Spiritual Exercises of St Ignatius* (St Louis Institute of Jesuit Sources, 1978), p. 71.
3. One, Catholic, Apostolic. Much of these sections is a reflection on three 'images' of working together: the Management Theory which suggests that a group has three functions (Maintaining Unity, Meeting Individual Needs and the Task); Jean Vanier's understanding (that a group needs bonding, caring and mission); and the role of abbot in the Benedictine community which Daniel Rees *et al.* suggest is to be the unitive centre, a representative of Christ and an educative guide in the life of the Spirit.
4. As we shall indicate later in the chapter, our baptism is our primary calling. Robin Greenwood, *Practising Community* (London, SPCK, 1996), writes:
   > So unity, once rooted in the security of conformity in an orthodox pattern of ordained ministry, has a more promising beginning in the act of baptism, the keystone for understanding the Christian experience of communion.
5. Jean Vanier, *Community and Growth* (London, DLT, 1989), pp. 42, 43.
6. *The ministry of healing is a gift given to the whole people of God. Some may have*

particular gifts to exercise in that setting, but no gift is to be exercised in a bizarre, quirky or individualistic way. The pointed question for any community to ask is this: Are we a body of people among whom those who are dis-eased will find healing, or is our common life in such dis-array that we shall block and hinder healing? (Jim Cotter, Healing – More or Less (Sheffield, 1987), p. 39)

7. Greenwood, p. 33:

   Regarding ordained ministry Lima asserts that to fulfil its mission the local church needs persons who are publicly and continually responsible for pointing to the fundamental dependence on Christ and therefore provide, through a diversity of gifts, a focus of unity.

8. *RB1980 The Rule of St Benedict in English* (Collegeville, Minnesota, The Liturgical Press, 1982), p. 95.
9. Greenwood, p. 39.
10. Dietrich Bonhoeffer, *Life Together* (London, SCM Press, 1954), p. 17.
11. Dietrich Bonhoeffer quoted in Esther de Waal, *Seeking God* (London, Fount, 1984), p. 139.
12. Daniel Rees *et al.*, *Consider Your Call* (London, SPCK, 1978), p. 87.
13. Vanier, *Community and Growth*, p. 166.
14. Joan Chittister, *The Rule of Benedict* (UK, St Pauls, 1992), p. 413.
15. At other times it will happen that people do not find the support they need within their particular community but will find it elsewhere, though still within the providence of God.
16. Vanier, *Community and Growth*, p. 48.
17. Bruno Bettelheim quoted in Vanier, *Community and Growth*, p. 90.
18. St Augustine.
19. Vanier, *Community and Growth*, p. 188.
20. *ABM Ministry Paper no. 1* (London, ABM, 1991), p. 42.
21. Rees, *et al.*, pp. 91f.
22. There is a stark contrast between this 'chosen' loneliness and the loneliness which is suffered as a result of inappropriate separation from the community. See Chapter 12 above.
23. *ABM Policy Paper no. 3b* (London, ABM, October 1993) Sect. D5.
24. See Chapters 5 and 11 above.
25. Jack Dominian quoted in Sr Eileen Mary SLG, *Saint Thérèse of Lisieux* (Oxford, SLG Press, 1997).
26. *ABM Ministry Paper no. 1*, pp. 31, 43.
27. Greenwood, p. 47.
28. *ABM Ministry Paper no. 1*, p. 39.
29. Vanier, *Community and Growth*, p. 248.
30. *ABM Ministry Paper no. 1*, pp. 7f and 34.
31. See section on Leadership in Chapter 12.
32. This last paragraph is very much a reflection of prayer rather than theology!
33. *ABM Ministry Paper no. 1*, p. 25.
34. ibid., p. 27.

35. From a consultation sponsored by the Edward King Institute for Ministry Development 1994 in Robin Greenwood, *Practising Community*, p. 5.
36. J. L. G. Balado, *The Story of Taizé* (Oxford, Mowbray, 1980), p. 85.
37. St Basil in George Guiver CR, *Pursuing the Mystery* (London, SPCK, 1996), p. 18.

14

Prophetic Vulnerability:
Worship

God created through love and for love. God did not create anything but love itself, and the means to love. He created love in all its forms. He created beings capable of love from all possible distances. Because nobody else could do it, he himself went to the greatest possible distance, the infinite distance. This infinite distance between God and God, this supreme tearing apart, this agony beyond all others, this marvel of love, is the crucifixion. Nothing can be further from God than that which is accursed.

This tearing apart over which supreme love places the bond of supreme union, echoes perpetually across the universe in the midst of the silence, like two notes, separate and yet melting into one, like pure and heart-rending harmony. This is the Word of God. The whole of creation is nothing but its vibration . . . those who persevere in love hear this note from the very lowest depths into which affliction has thrust them. From that moment they can no longer have any doubt.[1]

The image of two notes which resonate to sound the Word of God in the depth of our being is one which speaks profoundly to our subject. It is an image of the daily cross which Christ asks us to carry (Luke 9:23), a cross which Hans Küng describes:

Following the cross does not mean copying the suffering of Jesus, it is not the reconstruction of his cross. That would be presumptuous. But it certainly means enduring the suffering which befalls me in my inexchangeable situation –

in conformity with the suffering of Christ. Anyone who wants to go with Jesus must deny himself and take on himself not the cross of Jesus nor just any kind of cross, but his cross, his own cross, then he must follow Jesus.[2]

To live with our cross, to allow ourselves to resist the urge to make life tidy and safe, is to live with vulnerability. It is to understand that God is often heard not in the person who claims to have possession of unassailable truth but, rather, in the gentle voice of the one seeking for truth amidst the reality of life, the one who lives with the resonance of holding difference together.

In this chapter, we are exploring what vulnerability may mean in worship. We relate liturgy and worship to humankind's search for meaning and to the telling of story, personal and communal, within the wider story of salvation history. Against this background we look at some of the 'divine resonances' that may speak through worship, and at the place of word, sacrament, silence, music and art.

Liturgy

Perhaps the best definition of liturgy is the most all-embracing:

the liturgy is the Church's worship, and this means 'not the worship for which the Church has fixed the norms, nor the worship which the Church authorises; above all it means the worship which the Church actually does. The "Church at prayer" or the Church gathered for the activity of worship, is the real expression of the liturgy'.[3]

It is the community gathered for worship which concerns us in this chapter, the community which expects, and may have a burning desire, to meet Jesus in their midst in order to serve him in their lives, in each other, and in the wider settings of neighbourhood and world. Life and liturgy are held together in this transforming encounter with Jesus, the risen and exalted Lord, which resonates with the Lord we encounter as we serve our neighbours, or are served by them.

Liturgy, then, is a *present* reality. It is more than a dwelling on God's presence and action in the past. It is an expectation of his presence and action in the present, and often the birthplace of our response. Indeed, it is the place where Christ may be brought to birth in the soul. Eckhart tells us 'that the birth of God in the soul is God's uttering of his Word in the ground of the soul'.⁴

It is perhaps in this birth of God in the soul that we consent most profoundly to vulnerability, to being wounded and powerless, for love of God. There is then in worship a two-way encounter between God and the worshippers – individually and corporately. Worship is not only what we do, but what God is doing.

Our Search for Meaning

Viktor Frankl, reflecting on the experience of the concentration camps, writes, 'Man is not destroyed by suffering, he is destroyed by suffering without meaning.'⁵ We need meaning to give value and order to our way of living and being. Sometimes the meaning we give to our experience is the only choice left – but it is a choice and in the light of our faith we can review our experience, and, by allowing deeper meanings to emerge, often change the power of the past over us. For everything has meaning. Every event, each part of creation has *intrinsic* meaning, the meaning which God sees and for which we seek. They also have *extrinsic* meaning, that is, the meaning we give them which is no more than our current understanding. The way of vulnerability recognises that these meanings – the intrinsic God-given meaning and the extrinsic meaning (which may be different for each of us) – are not the same. To claim to know the ultimate meaning is to make an idol. This is certainly true of the way we treat many religious objects and even scripture itself. For example, we so easily take hold of the Bible, claiming to know the intrinsic meaning (God's meaning) and argue our corner rather than let the scriptures take hold of us. Perhaps we need, rather, to place ourselves in humility beneath God's revelation and not above it, opening ourselves to being wounded by all that he gives.

Like a scientist, we are constantly renewing our understandings as we change the extrinsic meaning we place on events. The intrinsic meaning which we seek may yet elude us and we may never fully be able to articulate it. To be faithful to this process is to risk another kind of vulnerability.

we experience a sort of bereavement when those formulations, images and symbols through which we had in the past appropriated truth have now to be abandoned. For those formulations, images and symbols, over the years become part of ourselves. . .[6]

The Place of 'Story'

The fact is that we find meaning in life not by looking at isolated events but by seeing their place in a narrative. Perhaps worship does this most when, somehow, it provides the ladder 'betwixt Heaven and Charing Cross', when Christ is 'walking on the water, Not of Gennesareth, but Thames',[7] that is, when it makes connections between our living and our praying so that our worship is part of the flow of our lives. It is, then, when our worship and our prayer can relate *our* story to the *gospel* story and the *gospel* story to *our* story, that we know that we are on a journey which is also Christ's journey and not some other. It is then, however painful it may be, that we see in our living the presence of Christ. Wilfred Owen writes of inspecting conscripts:

For fourteen hours yesterday I was at work, teaching Christ to lift his cross by numbers and how to adjust his crown . . . I attended his supper to see that there were no complaints; and inspected the feet to see that they should be worthy of nails.[8]

It is in such incidents, when the gospel story and the reality of life touch each other, that we may gain insight into the mystery of God, of our neighbour and of our own being. For a moment, we touch a deeper reality and, in the touching, recognise that to do so is not an ending but a beginning. Touching the reality of God is like stepping through a breach in a high wall to discover a vast open space. As you exhaust the exploration of the spaciousness and the liberality of his love, and maybe of his pain, you discover another breach in another wall, a greater spaciousness and giftedness – mystery always giving way to mystery.

In an age of paradox, an age of both increasing alienation from and yet greater concern for the natural world, an age where the illusion of soap opera is sometimes more compelling than the reality of our own lives, worship may enable people to become aware of the divine in their daily lives.

Only Connect! That was the whole of her sermon. Only connect the prose and the passion, and both will be exalted and human love will be seen at its height. Live in fragments no longer.[9]

And 'connect' is not necessarily to understand or explain. It is to dare to bring together.

Divine Resonances

In Chapter 13 we suggested that the nature of the Trinity, being perichoretic, was reflected in the Christian community by clergy and laity each encouraging the other to be faithful to their own unique vocation. The fundamental vocation for all is to be true to the self that God sees in us – not then to level our differences but to hold them together and listen for the divine resonances.[10] In this way, unavoidable tensions and our differences can be held together creatively, allowing them to be places of revelation rather than confrontation and division.

What then might some of these tensions, these differences, be, and how are they manifested in worship? Here are some examples, by no means exhaustive, but enough to communicate the theme of living creatively with vulnerability *in the tension* and, through them, being open to being wounded and changed.

Liturgy/Life

George Guiver CR argues that,

Liturgy and life cannot often be brought very closely together. Then the vital surprise, the interillumination, is lost. It is not possible normally to import much of daily life into the liturgy or vice versa, because we are dealing with a chemistry which happens between them.[11]

It is an interesting view, and one which bears much thought. There is, of course, a need for liturgy and life to encounter one another. At times though, it is enough that the encounter is only articulated in the intercessions and the Sermon. The encounter is already there in the gathered community. If we could see on a screen the lives and experience gathered at any one service, we would hesitate to add much more 'encounter'. Too much changing of the liturgy in an effort to force a sense of 'encounter' may only serve to disempower those gathered, preventing them from placing their story alongside salvation history. At other times, the service will rightly focus on the corporate encounter with an issue or theme. There is a balance to be found.

Universal/Particular

We have already argued that it is right to attend both to the universal Church and the local community, to both the general and the particular. This balance is constantly to be addressed in respect of the Church's worship. We may take three examples.

Firstly, the debate about who should celebrate the Eucharist. The debate about women priests, was, for some, about maintaining our links with the universal Church, and those who otherwise may have been in agreement with the change found they could not agree because of this concern. It is a fair comment and one which we respect; yet in the light of what we are saying, another view can be examined. Our understanding of the Trinity is that the members of the Trinity affirm each other's identity by their relationship of love and trust. Their difference within that relationship is gift to each other and to us. In the community of the world Church, the Church of England, coming to its own discernment of the 'mind of Christ' and being true to that discernment, is not – at a deep level – a challenge to unity, but can be a gift, in love, which might set others free.

Secondly, we may take the issue of liturgical revision. Liturgy is, of course, more than words, though, in legislative terms, words are most easily proscribed. The provision of choice within liturgy is, therefore, essential if the whole of the Church of England is to use a single overall 'package' of services. What is not so easily bound by legislation is the ritual and gestures used in the liturgy. Without care, particularity in this area soon gives way to idiosyncrasy. Acknowledging different strands of tradition in the Church of England, it may yet be possible to agree a number of 'styles' of leading worship which makes gesture more universal and may include the whole community.

Thirdly, worship has to be contextualised. A friend talks of the shock of singing 'Onward Christian Soldiers' in Tamil. It is more than words which need translation. It is music and shape, style and gesture so that the liturgy is accessible to those who worship whilst maintaining a commonality with the universal Church.

Control/Freedom

The idea of gesture takes us on to another 'tension', that is, the tension between explaining what we are doing and letting worship speak for itself. We shall come to this when we look at words and symbols. The point is that we cannot control God and what he will do through his liturgy. The explanation that makes sense to us may not be at all helpful to others, or the difference itself may be a point of illumination. Rabbi Lionel Blue reminds us, as only he could, that God is not to be controlled:

> It takes two to tango in human love, and with divine love it's no different. It's not just a case of you doing your own thing, it's also a case of the Almighty doing His (or Her) own thing, and unless you synchronise you get nowhere. People come and complain, 'Rabbi, I went to the synagogue service, I said all the right prayers, I didn't walk out during the sermon and what happened – nothing.' They obviously want to swear at you know Whom, but feel a bit uncertain, and just bottle up their crossness and take it out on their family instead. It happens to me too. I make an appointment to meet God at eleven o'clock on a Saturday morning in such-and-such a place of worship. I arrive early. I say all the right things. I stand up, sit down and stand up again. I bow here, I bow there and bow-wow in all the right places, but I don't wow Him because He (or She) doesn't show up, and I'm left holding a Prayer Book talking to nobody.[12]

Glory/Suffering

In vulnerability learned from Christ it [the apostolic church] is known for its ability and willingness to be companions with the weak and marginalised in society.[13]

In sharing in the life of Christ, we are to share both in his suffering and in his resurrection. Both will need to find expression in worship if we are to reveal Christ in need and in glory to one another. Perhaps the most striking reflection is that of people who, thinking back over years, realise how often they had been encouraged to find an end to suffering, and how seldom they had been encouraged to find meaning in unavoidable suffering, or ways of allowing God to use it in their life. Mary Craig, a mother of four boys, two of whom were born disabled – Paul with gargoylism and Nicky with mongolism – found that the birth of Nicky brought her to a place where she says 'I was left vulnerable and when one is vulnerable one has the ability to learn', discovering that

the value of suffering does not lie in the pain of it, which is morally neutral, but in what the sufferer makes of it. Two persons can go through the same anguish; one of them may be destroyed by it, the other may achieve an extra dimension. The real tragedy . . . is the wasted opportunity.

She suggests:

Human beings have a deep need for stillness and harmony. In the standing still, in the acceptance of the *unavoidable* moment in all its bleakness, lies the possibility of salvation and growth for ourselves and for others. (our italics)[14]

To be sharing in the κοινωσια, 'koinonia' of Christ's suffering (Phil. 3:10) is to hold our suffering with his, our suffering alongside that of the world; so redemption becomes, *in him*, our work too.

Glory may shine through suffering but it comes too in many other guises. In our opening quotation Simone Weil spoke of the Word of God sounding from two notes, separate yet melting into one. In this is glory revealed.

> I saw God today,
>   I held him.
>   I held him twice.

I found him in a
  piece of bread,
    broken,
      broken body,
nails and blood,
  and pain,
    piercing to my heart
      and filling me with love.

I found him in a baby boy,
  a gift of God,
    a baby born of love –
of human parents,
  and a Father's care.
I held him,
  held this child,
recognised his Father,
  caught the glance,
the love,
  in Joseph's face,
    'trailing clouds of glory
      as he came from God,
        who is his home.'

I saw beyond the baby's face
  and saw the face of Christ,
    tears streaming down my face,
      love piercing to the heart
and I am whole again.[15]

Head/Heart and Awesome Mystery/Loving Mystery

In an age where psychology has revealed to us, with some clarity, that we all have different temperaments, liturgy needs to be created that holds space for both thinking and feeling. Liturgy may also be informed by the different needs of the person who is naturally reflective and the one who is naturally active. In himself, Jesus holds together the *awesome* mystery (the events where he stands alone in glory: Transfiguration, Gethsemane, Crucifixion, Resurrection, Ascension) and the *loving* mystery (the Jesus who washes feet). In worship as encounter with the living Jesus, we may expect to see him in all his guises, for somehow worship finds a transparency and becomes a window into the divine.

Encounter/Enclosure[16]

In worship, as in the whole of the life of the community, there is a need to nourish the faith of the long-term member as well as nurture the faith of the people who have only recently turned to God. There may be those present who as yet are still searching too. A variety of worship with different emphases may be necessary.

Pickled in the Word

The spirituality of the ordained person is a spirituality of that ever living and ever acting word. It is the spirituality of one who hears the word, studies the word, ponders the word, prays the word, teaches the word, preaches the word at the highest level of sacramental intensity, brings the word into every area of human living, and lives the word.

So writes Thomas Lane CM.[17] It is the word which shapes us all, clergy and laity alike. To be 'pickled in the word' is to allow it to seep into the cells and fibres of our being, no longer a surface knowledge of the word which causes division but that deeper reception of the word which brings healing and revelation. We need to be pickled like onions which have soaked in vinegar until every layer of life is imbued with the aroma and the living love of Christ.

Words in worship can transform. Simply reading scripture well in the context of liturgy is both privilege and gift. Matthew Arnold remarked of Newman that he had 'the most entrancing of voices, breaking the silence with words and thoughts which were a religious movement, subtle, sweet mournful'. Others noted how his reading of the lesson brought new meaning to the words.[18] All words used in worship need handling with care. Words have a power of deception. A half-remembered song says 'take from us our words that sound full of peace but are only subtle weapons to separate us from each other'. We need to be discerning in our use of words, to use them wisely to make connections rather than to divide, to build bridges rather than barriers. We need words that are transparent to the Word. We need to use words which are windows to life and to God, not sentimentally pious words, but holy words. We need to engage with society not just to *appear* relevant but so that, deeply engaged, critically engaged, we may be open and receptive to Christ's ministry through us to the world.

We need to hear the words of those who gaze at God and who experience the resonances of life deep within. We listen to them as they dare to say what they have begun to perceive, words said hesitantly, offered rather than forced, words that as St Cyril says, do not 'set limits to the infinite'.[19]

The preacher must first draw from secret prayer what he will later pour out in holy sermons. He must first grow hot within before he speaks words that themselves are cold.[20]

The preacher who dares to be a channel of God's word is vulnerable – vulnerable to self-doubts and questioning, to people's misunderstanding and criticism, to tiredness and being drained. None of this prevents God using us, providing we allow it all to be transparent to him, providing that we give him access. The preacher is struggling, perhaps, with the tension between the extrinsic meaning of the words he speaks and his own experience of the intrinsic meaning of life in Christ. To put that into words is rightly a struggle. The struggle is not a sign of weakness but a recognition, in awe, of the commission and the responsibility.

No one who preaches will underestimate the vulnerability of preaching after a great disaster. The words of Dietrich Bonhoeffer say it all: 'Where God tears great gaps in our lives we should not try to fill them with human words,'[21] and yet something needs to be said. People need meaning. 'He who has a *why* to live by can cope with almost any *how*.'[22] The meaning cannot be imposed, but the preacher can come alongside and explore in the light of faith. In 1989 Rt Revd James Whyte preached at the Lockerbie Memorial Service. He said:

When we cry in our pain, we cry to the one who knows pain, who shares it with us. That is strange comfort, but it may give it meaning as with a flash of light.[23]

Sustained by Sacraments

To try to explain the Sacraments is immediately to risk limiting them. Of the Eucharist Christopher Nolan writes: 'God assumed beautiful credit by breathing love through the Eucharist;'[24] and Jeremy Taylor comments, 'The sacraments do something in the hand of God.'[25]

As we leave the medieval distortions behind – the clericalism, the taking over of the roles of the laity by the priest[26] – we may allow the Eucharist to speak for itself, to be the place where the community is fed, sustained and nourished by the Father, as Christ presents himself to us in the power of the Spirit. Like all worship, the Eucharist needs careful, not fussy, preparation, so that it may be left to be what God would have it be.

To say mass better every day will be to say it more simply every day, each day with one less crease in your brow and one less anxiety in your head and one less shadow of fear in your heart.[27]

Blessed by Beauty

God created all things and all things can be a means to worship. What matters is how we use silence, symbol, sound and stage to enhance that worship and to become imaginative and creative vehicles through which God may meet with us and we with him.

Silence

Words about God are not to be despised. But when words are done there is still more, unsaid, in the silence.[28]

Silence can so easily convey what words cannot, but silence in worship can bring its own vulnerability. It does need 'shaping', for silence becomes communication when it has an expectation, when we are absorbed, whether it be in grief for a person, or in some object of beauty, or God. In this contemplative silence, we become vulnerable to true meaning – to the is-ness of things, to their intrinsic worth, and often to that deep-down hidden joy.

Symbols

Meaning is also conveyed in symbols, and especially in those symbols which are allowed to find their *own* meaning in people's lives. Symbols speak differently to each of us. If we try too earnestly to express the meaning of a symbol, we may 'limit the infinite'. We need to let *God* speak, and when God speaks in symbols, he often uses them to hold together people who hold very different understandings. God uses symbols in this way for we are ultimately held together not by words but by love, by a man on a cross 'in stillness nailed to hold all time, all change, all circumstance in Love's embrace'.[29]

Art, Music and Drama

In worship, there is often scope for embracing beauty and action, shape and colour to create worship which speaks powerfully of our response to God and of his gifts, or to draw us to prayer. For example, we read earlier of Wilfred Owen inspecting the feet of conscripts. Placing those words alongside Stanley Spencer's painting *The Last Supper* (1920) may encourage a deepening of prayer. Or again, it is said that St Ignatius came to an understanding of the Trinity by hearing three notes played first separately and then together in harmony.[30] In itself it is a wonderful image but, for some, gazing at Rublev's ikon of the Trinity deepens it, and playing Arvo Pärt's 'Spiegel im Spiegel' for violin and piano deepens it further. Worship requires imagination and restraint – another divine resonance.

Vulnerable to Life

Perhaps the one service, widely shared, which showed such imagination and restraint was that held for the funeral of Diana, Princess of Wales. Reflecting on her death and on her ability, in life, to come alongside those who suffer, Bishop Richard Harries writes:

so many people's lives are in a mess, particularly people under 35, and the way to communicate with them is by being vulnerable, by sharing something of our own dilemmas and pain.[31]

It was certainly so, and right that Princess Diana's funeral portrayed that vulnerability in its simplicity. It drew together many of our themes: the long procession, the silence shaped by a tolling bell, by words and by a breadth of music which together reflected not only the love that many felt for this vulnerable individual, but also held the pain they experienced at her untimely death. It has been said that the service did not allow for a proclaiming of the gospel in the way we might have wished. Yet when love and pain are held together in silence, there is a resonance of Christ, holding all in Love's embrace, and for those with ears to hear, the Word is speaking. There is a weeping too, the weeping of the Christ who had suffered with and for her, and who, as at the grave of Lazarus, surely wept for her. And in *him* even weeping can be worship.[32]

In this chapter we have explored the rich texture of a worship which embraces vulnerability. We have suggested that we need to listen to divine resonances in our different approaches and styles and not lose the gifts that God offers by a bland uniformity. We have gently appealed for imagination and restraint.

A few weeks ago, Churches Together in England announced that they will be manufacturing 25 million candles to be lit at 11.58 p.m. on December 31st 1999. At the time I thought it was a silly idea which wouldn't catch on. Now I'm not so sure. But it will only work if the churches abandon their colourless services and lead people where they want to go: into an imaginative landscape of mystery and symbol where time itself is sacred.

Damian Thompson, The Times, 13 September 1997

NOTES

1. Simone Weil, *Waiting on God* (Glasgow, Collins, 1951), pp. 82–3.
2. Hans Küng, *On Being a Christian* (Glasgow, Fount, 1977), p. 777.
3. Joseph Jungmann quoted in George Guiver CR, *Pursuing the Mystery* (London,

SPCK, 1996), p. 125. This book by George Guiver CR has been very much one note that sounds with the other note (of experience) between them producing this chapter.

4. Oliver Davies, *Meister Eckhart: Selected Writings* (London, Penguin, 1994), p. xxvii.

5. Victor Frankl, *Man's Search for Meaning* (London, Hodder & Stoughton, 1964).

6. Donald Nicholl, *The Beatitude of Truth* (London, DLT, 1997), p. 6. See Austin Farrer quotation in Chapter 12, p. 140.

7. Francis Thompson, *Selected Poems* (London, Burns & Oates, 1909), p. 130. 'In no strange land'.

8. Dominic Hibberd, *Wilfred Owen – The Last Year* (London, Constable, 1992).

9. E. M. Forster, *Howards End* (London, The Folio Society, 1973), Chapter 22.

10. See, for example, *ABM Ministry Paper no. 1*: 'By arriving at a clearer sense of institutional identity the Church of England will be *more* effective in ecumenical endeavours' (p. 25). It is by a clearer sense of difference that that deeper meaning can be revealed.

11. Guiver, p. 99.

12. Lionel Blue, *Bright Blue* (BBC Books) quoted in Ivan Mann, *The Golden Key* (Northampton, MNDA, 1990), p. 29.

13. Robin Greenwood, *Practising Community* (London, SPCK, 1996), p. 54.

14. Mary Craig, *Blessings* (London, Hodder & Stoughton, 1979) NB 'unavoidable': this is vital to grasp – we are not valuing suffering for its own sake. To return to the quotation from Hans Küng at the beginning of the chapter, we are talking here of the cross which we carry, the suffering which cannot be relieved.

15. Ivan Mann, 'On seeing a friend's baby for the first time', a piece written standing alongside the father of the child as we shared in worship.

16. See Chapter 13.

17. Thomas Lane CM, *A Priesthood in Tune* (Dublin, The Columba Press, 1993), p. 206.

18. Norman White, *Hopkins* (Oxford, Clarendon Press, 1992), p. 44.

19. St Cyril of Alexandria, *c.* 400 AD.

20. St Francis, further source unknown.

21. Edwin Robertson, *The Shame and the Sacrifice* (London, Hodder & Stoughton, 1987), p. 177.

22. Nietzsche quoted in Frankl.

23. *The Times*, 5 January 1989.

24. Christopher Nolan, *Under the Eye of the Clock* (London, Weidenfeld & Nicolson, 1987), p. 60.

25. Jeremy Taylor quoted in Kenneth Stevenson, *Covenant of Grace Renewed* (London, DLT, 1994), p. 173.

26. Church of England GS 512 (London, CBF, 1997).

27. Thomas Merton, *The Sign of Jonas* (London, Hollis & Charter, 1953).

28. Gerald Priestland, *Priestland's Progress* (London, BBC, 1981), p. 9.

29. Gilbert Shaw in Mother Mary Clare SLG, *The Apostolate of Prayer* (Oxford, SLG Press, 1972), p. 15.

30. Philip Caraman SJ, *Ignatius Loyola* (London, Collins, 1990), pp. 113, 160.

31. Richard Harries, *The Tablet*, 20/27 December 1997.

32. Luke 7:36–end, for example.

15

Vulnerability:
'Place me with your Son'[1]

But how is one to explain the tears of Ignatius? No other mystic has wept so much. His intimate friend Laynez tells us that ordinarily he wept six or seven times a day. His eyesight was endangered by the abundance of tears.

Mystics often speak of a deeply spiritual experience that overflows on the senses. They speak of an inner fire, a blind stirring of love, a living flame of love which is so powerful that it causes the stigmata, the five wounds of Jesus, or other physical phenomena such as rapture or ecstasy or dislocation of the bones. Ignatius did not experience such phenomena. Instead he shed tears. In a person of his temperament tears were the outer expression of his deeply spiritual interior experience.[2]

As we come to the final chapter of this book, it seems appropriate that we should take off our authors' hats and 'come clean'. Rather than simply write in an objective way about the way of vulnerability, we should remove *our* masks, and share something of the story behind what we have tried to articulate in the preceding pages. Not that we are very far along the way; but we can begin to see how God has led us, and it is our prayer that he will use our limited experience to encourage others on that way.

Vanessa Writes . . .

This book is the product of experience. It began twenty years ago, in the lived experience of an Anglican clergyman. It was formed and moulded in the interior experience of one who discovered that leadership in the Christian community demanded more than he had anticipated. It found its roots amid the security of loving friends whose accompaniment allowed risks to be taken and truth to be revealed. It began to emerge in that leader's willingness to take the risk of beginning to walk the way of vulnerability. That leader was Ivan.

The genesis of the project was a month's placement in the parish where Ivan was priest, as part of my ordination training. For each of us the experience was a catalyst. For me it was about encountering and exploring a completely new model of leading.

It became clear very soon after my placement had begun, that the leadership model which I saw in Ivan was different from any that I had encountered before. Here was a parish priest effectively fulfilling the normal and expected duties of any incumbent – planning and leading worship, pastoral ministry both within and beyond the congregation, involvement in the parish community (especially in the church school), spiritual direction, and the variety of administrative and management tasks associated with a large and active church – yet his approach was somehow refreshingly and strikingly different.

As we explored what this difference might be about, we focused on three factors which seemed to be foundational to the model of leadership with which I was confronted: firstly, Ivan's understanding of priesthood; secondly, Ivan's desire in ministry to be 'transparent to Christ'; and thirdly, his understanding of Christian leadership as built on a life of prayer, vulnerability and trust, rather than relevance, popularity and power. Each of these needs some amplification.

Priesthood

Ivan's understanding of priesthood may be summarised as follows: all priesthood is Christ's; Christ shares that priesthood with all believers; some are called to function as leaders within that corporate priesthood to serve and enable others in the task of ministry to the world.

Transparency

Christ's priesthood was one of *disclosure*, that is, he revealed in and through his ministry *who he was*. This should be the pattern of our priesthood; we should reveal Christ, that is *be transparent to him*, and in so doing be freed to become and to reveal our true selves. There is no place for hiding behind a role and so limiting Christ's revelation of himself through us.

Prayer, Vulnerability and Trust

In his book *In the Name of Jesus*,[3] Henri Nouwen reflects on the Temptations of Jesus (Matt. 4:1–11) and Peter's call to be a shepherd (John 21:15–19). He urges Christian leaders to resist the temptation to be relevant, spectacular and powerful, but rather, through the disciplines of contemplative prayer, confession, forgiveness and theological reflection, to be leaders who are:

(i) knowingly loved by God and in love with him;

(ii) willing to be vulnerable to others;

(iii) willing to abandon power and control over their lives and ministries in order to be led by Christ in all things.

It was something of this approach to leadership which I saw in Ivan, and which caused me to reassess my understanding and expectations of what it meant to be one who was currently being trained for ordination. I took the opportunity, during the course of the placement, to try to find out what effect such a style of leadership had on the parish.

Observations and conversations with a wide variety of people highlighted a number of areas in which Ivan's leadership model appeared to have a direct effect – sometimes positive, sometimes negative – on members of the congregation. One was in the area of worship, the other pastoral care. When leading worship, Ivan himself was often deeply moved: tears would well up in his eyes, and when praying (and even preaching) he would sometimes be so 'touched by Christ' that he would have to pause and re-compose himself in order to continue leading.

Not surprisingly, the congregation responded to this style of leadership in different ways. For some, this emotional intensity, vulnerability and spontaneity released them to enter deeply into worship themselves; for others, the apparent lack of predictability and Ivan's apparent lack of control (we might even say lack of 'professionalism') led to strong feelings of alienation and insecurity. The cynical observer might suggest that Ivan's leading was highly manipulative. It would be wrong to suggest that the worship was out of control – but it certainly made some members of the congregation feel confused and uncomfortable.

Ivan had a strong ministry of pastoral care towards members of the congregation. A good proportion of his time was spent in working with people individually, and his ministry (both pastorally and in spiritual direction) was obviously appreciated. His passionate love for Christ overflowed in a deep love for people which he demonstrated not through a ministry of 'problem-solving' but rather through staying alongside people in their pain, through listening, touch and prayer, both 'one-to-one' and (with members of the prayer team) through the ministry of laying on of hands and anointing which was offered after each service. Much healing took place.

There seemed to be a continuity, however, between people's reactions to Ivan's style of leading worship and their willingness to approach him for pastoral care. Those who responded positively to his vulnerability seemed able to trust him with *their* vulnerability; those who felt alienated by him seemed reluctant to approach him with their needs. They were, perhaps, seeking a safer, more detached 'professional' approach, which would, in a sense, be less threatening to *them*. This is not to suggest that Ivan was *unprofessional* in his dealings with people! My observations of his ministry through the occasional offices and in the wider context of the parish suggested that his ministry was both appropriate and well-received. It was some of those within the congregation who struggled most!

Working alongside Ivan challenged my perception of Christian leadership, and raised many questions for me concerning 'professionalism' and vulnerability in those who are leaders in the Christian community; in particular, how people respond to that vulnerability and whether it can be destructive as well as upbuilding.

Although my experience raised questions, it was a deep and personally challenging one. It is now nearly three years since that placement. In the meantime, I have completed my ordination training and been ordained deacon and priest. I have had the opportunity to explore – both through theological study and personal experience – what it means to try to walk the way of vulnerability, following the self-emptying Christ. It seems clear to me that there is no other way to follow.

Ivan Writes . . .

but only with trepidation. Bérulle makes the point that Jesus only wrote in the sand and even that is not recorded.[4] We speak of these things, then, not to suggest we have answers but because we believe that they point us to Jesus. In my years of ministry I have made many mistakes. What keeps me going in faith is a passionate love for Jesus, a love which often moves me to tears. I may be in a different league but I am in good company. St Ambrose, for example, writes of his love for Christ:

Thus we have everything in Christ. Let every soul go to Him, whether he be sick from the sins of the body, or pierced with the nails of some desire of this age; or still imperfect – provided that it goes forward in persevering meditation, or is already perfect in many virtues: everything is within Christ's power, and Christ is everything to us. If you wish to be healed of your wound, He is the healer; if you burn with fevers, He is the fountain; if you are laden with iniquity, He is justice; if you have need of help, He is strength; if you fear death; he is life; if you desire heaven, He is the way to it; if you flee from darkness he is the light; if you seek food He is nourishment. 'Taste, then, and see how good is the Lord: happy the man who hopes in Him.'[5]

What Vanessa has not explained is that she used her experience of being placed with God's Son in vulnerability to read for an MA. Towards the end of 1996 she brought her dissertation to show me. As I read some of her comments (much as she has given them

above) I found myself wanting to respond. My response came out in
suggesting this book and, later, in writing this:

Is there a choice?
   Can I not love?
      can I not gaze upon his face
and fall again in love?
can I *choose* to let tears flow,
   to make them stop
when, gazing on his face, his eyes
I find myself absorbed in love?
Can I walk away?
      It would be to choose to die.
O Yes, there are times
when for love of Him
     I hold myself from gazing
        in order to serve His way

 – contain myself
      that others may be free.
But to choose to turn away
rather than RISK
     rather than LIVE
    would be to die
       would be *the* sin.
So let me gaze on Him
    and let Him choose.
Let Him water love with tears,
   or hold them back.
Let me listen to His voice,
  His will
     – to risk or to contain,
       to overflow with love,
         or take the quiet stance
           of waiting.
His will, not mine be done.
  His love,
    His joy,

          His peace
be what others see,
    not me.
Let me be as glass –
    transparent to His being
        open and vulnerable to His love,
           complete surrender.
This is my desire,
    Nothing more.
        Nothing less.
This is my desire –
    Christ, and him alone,
        Nothing, nothing but Him.

What then of the parish experience? For me, the key to my experience there is found in Jean Vanier's comment that

love makes us weak and vulnerable because it breaks down the barriers and protective armour we have built around ourselves. Love means letting others reach us and being sensitive enough to reach them.[6]

I went to the parish already used to the idea of living vulnerably. My first wife had died after five years' illness, leaving me with four children. I had married again (to Catherine) and we have a further two children, but the experience of looking after Jackie and four small ones had already stripped me in many ways. When I was interviewed for the parish I met the churchwardens. I found in them an enormous love and depth of faith. I recognised Christ in them. More than anything else, their attitude made me feel the parish was right. From other perspectives, there were questions for me about style and a recognition that I would be very vulnerable there. Coming to a decision took some time in discernment but, once made, the choice felt and continues to feel right.

What I found when I arrived was a wealth of love and friendship that I have seldom known, and the stripping which had not yet been done began. It exposed an enormous love, and an enormous pain – consider again Simone Weil's 'two notes'.[7] Living with the resonance,

I came to a deeper faith, and a greater depth of love for Christ. I
wrote:

> At the heart of my being
>   is love.
> In silence I allow the
>   mists to clear
>   and slowly, gently
>   the face of love
> – it is the face of Christ –
> comes clear
>   and living water
>   begins to well up
>   unbidden
>   in my soul
> and I am filled
> with light and love and joy . . .
>   and for that time
> – maybe only the blinking of an eye,
>   but eternity to me –
>   I am home.

As before in Chapter 14 where I wrote about holding young Joseph
and knowing Christ in him, the experience was a coming home, but
it was only one of the two notes that were sounding. It became clear
that there was also a note of pain which even when I spoke of love
others would hear. We wrote in Chapter 4 that 'Sometimes, however,
"the pain speaks for itself"'. There were two components of the pain:
a note of pain from my own journey and also the pain of sensing a
call from God to move on. For a long time I resisted it, but then
realised I had to listen. At about the same time my present post was
advertised, and I and others felt it right that I apply for it. It was a
time of learning much about the necessity of wearing masks, a desert
experience of doubting that my approach to ministry had any validity,
but through that experience, of which writing this book has been a
part, it has been affirmed and clarified. Vanessa has written that the
experience of the placement was a catalyst for both of us. For me,
her coming and our subsequent collaboration has given me the

freedom to articulate the reality of my lived experience both as a priest and indeed before my ordination. Quite simply, Vanessa has given voice to my song. I remain aware of and grateful for the love that stripped me (both human and divine) of the costliness of choosing to remain vulnerable, and of my unwillingness to suggest that others should walk this way!

Yes, I have made a choice – a conscious one – to be with Christ wherever he may be, but I would never try to be vulnerable. It would be false, like trying to be other than I am. No, the way of vulnerability is not like that at all. It is not about making an effort to be religious in this particular way. It is rather to discover that you become vulnerable to God (you consent to his way for you) only to discover that you become vulnerable to people too.

Vanessa has described tears. Experience reveals that tears often flow when reality touches. They are not however the tears of emotion; often people say that they experience no great emotion with this gift of tears.[8] What they do experience is a sense of touching on divine reality and, in that, the reality of the human condition. In this, as in all things, there is a time and a season, a time for tears and a time to cease from tears. Discernment is all.

But Jesus wept. I came across a wonderful picture of the Church of Dominus Flevit. It is said to be built on the spot where Jesus wept over Jerusalem. Behind the altar is a window overlooking the city. Only as I gazed at the picture did I realise that as Jesus looked over Jerusalem he would be looking over the Garden of Gethsemane. Perhaps it was already a favourite place for prayer. Perhaps he knew it would be his place of succour as the events leading to his death unfolded, a place where olive trees might shelter him, and the Father's feathers surround him (see Luke 13:34; Ps. 91), the place where he would consent to the Father's way. Here, in the place of tears, is also the place of consent.

In Joyful Collaboration, We Say . . .

Our desire, our choosing, is summed up in the words of St Ignatius. All we desire is that God place us with his Son. Vulnerability is simply the consequence.

> *If we are to be followers of His way, then our greatness is measured not just by our service to the powerless, but by our total identification with them. We are to become one with their feelings, their thoughts, their reality. When we do this, we become as little children: open, vulnerable, and trusting, a terrifying prospect for any of us raised to survive as the fittest. But it is our call, our task as Christians . . . to be a servant people, a servant church, like children in our openness, to others, like children in our vulnerability to others, like children in our trust in others: We are to become like the ones we serve. And the promise is that when we live like this, we will release something very deep and personal, something that has been within us from our own childhood: We will release God within, transforming the world with our vulnerable greatness.*[9]

AMEN   AMEN   AMEN

NOTES

1. Ignatius 'prayed to our Lady to put him with her son, to be received under the standard of the Lord and Saviour and be totally accepted into his companionship'. Philip Caraman, *Ignatius Loyola* (London, Collins, 1990), p. 113.

2. William Johnston, *Mystical Theology: The Science of Love* (London, Fount/Harper Collins, 1996), p. 338.

3. Henri Nouwen, *In the Name of Jesus: Reflections on Christian Leadership* (London, DLT, 1989).

4. Quoted in Louis Bouyer, *A Christian History of Spirituality*, Vol. 1 (Tunbridge Wells, Burns & Oates, 1969), p. 35.

5. Bouyer, p. 458.

6. Jean Vanier, *Community and Growth* (London, DLT, 1989), p. 48.

7. See the beginning of Chapter 14.

8. See, for example, Caraman, p. 160: 'The most excellent tears are those that come from the thought and love of the Divine Persons.'

9. Will Leckie and Barry Stopfel, *Courage to Love* (New York, Doubleday, 1997).

Index of Names

Adam 68
Allan P., 120, 130
Ambrose, St 8, 179
Anna 10, 30
Arnold, Matthew 169
Augustine of Hippo, St 7, 158
Autton, Norman 59

Bailey, Kenneth 19
Balado, J. L. G. 159
Barth, Karl ch. 2 *passim*, 70
Basil, St 159
Bauckham, R. 88
Baxter, Christina 142
Benedict XV, Pope 71
Benedict, St ch. 6 *passim*, 78, 81, 142, 145, 157, 158
Bettelheim, Bruno 158
Bloom, Anthony 58, 59
Blue, Lionel 22, 34, 166, 174
Bonhoeffer, Dietrich 133, 141, 142, 147, 158, 170
Borger, Robert 130
Bouyer, Louis 184
Bowker, John 112, 116
Broderick, William 71
Brown, Raymond E. 81
Bérulle 179

Campbell, Alistair V. 59, ch. 10 *passim*
Campbell, J. Y. 59

Caraman, Philip 174, 184
Carr, Wesley 115
Carthusian, A 33, 34, 71
Cassidy, Sheila 59
Chadwick, Owen 34
Chittister, Joan 70, 71, 142, 158
Coggan, Donald 77, 81, 86, 88
Cotter, Jim 67, 71, 99, 158
Craig, Mary 167, 174
Cyril of Alexandria, St 170, 174

Davies, Oliver 174
De Chantal, St Jane 62, 70
De Foucauld, Charles 34, 100
Delfieux, Pierre-Marie 141, 142
de Sales, St Francis 70
de Waal, Esther 158
Diana, Princess of Wales ix, 172, 173
Dominian, Jack 92, 99, 151, 158

Eckhart, Meister 162, 174
Eileen Mary, Sister 158
Elijah 27
Eliot, T. S. 93, 99
English, John 135, 139, 142

Farrer, Austin 142, 174
Fleming, David 157
Forster, E. M. 174
Francis of Assisi, St 174
Frankl, Victor 81, 162, 174

Index of Names

Ganss, George E. 81
Gardner, Helen 19
Garlaandt, J. G. 28
General Synod of the Church of
England 130
Glasse, James 104, 114
Gore, Charles 18
Gorree, George 34
Grayston, K. 108, 115
Greenwood, Robin 142, ch. 13 *passim*
Guerric of Igny, St 91, 99
Guiver, George 37, 159, 164, 173, 174
Gunton, C. 19, 48

Hammarskjöld, Dag 20, 31, 33, 34
Harries, Richard ix, 172, 174
Hibberd, Dominic 174
Hillesum, Etty 27, 34
Holloway, Richard 59, 110, 115
Hopkins, G. M. 174

Ignatius of Loyola, St 61, 70, 81, 95,
157, 172, 175, 184
Irenaeus, St 7

Jairus 106
James, St 27, 38
Jeremias, Joachim, 23, 24
Jerome, St 52, 90
John Chrysostom, St 52, 59
John of the Cross, St 91, 95, 99
John the Apostle, St 27, 38
John the Baptist, St 15, 21, 22, 25, 58,
106, 145, 153
Johnston, William 34, 184
Joseph, St 10, 22, 58
Judas Iscariot 80, 143, 147
Julian of Norwich 88
Jüngmann, Joseph 173

Kavanaugh, K. 99
Kierkegaard, S. 93
Kirsty, Sister 92, 93, 99
Küng, Hans 99, 160, 173, 174

Lane, Thomas 99, 169, 174
Laynez, Diego 175
Lazarus ch. 10 *passim*, 173
Leckie, Will 184
Leech, Kenneth 118, 119, 130
Lovell, George 81
Lucas, Catherine 62, 70

Mann, Ivan 34, 89, 99, 174
Mary, Blessed Virgin 10, 13, 22, 29, 58,
61, 68, 184
Mary Clare, Mother 71, 174
Mary and Martha, SS 34, 107, 108
McCann, Justin 81
Merton, Thomas 124, 130, 142, 174
Metz, Johannes 63, 70
Middleton, J. R. 48
Milner-White, Eric 17
Milton, John 72, 80
Moltmann, Jurgen 85, 88
Moody, Christopher 109, 115
Morrell, J. H. L. 116
Moses 22, 27
Muir, Edwin 61, 70

Nain, Widow of 30, 106
Newbolt, W. C. E. 116
Newman, John Henry 169
Nicholl, Donald 174
Nietzsche, Friedrich 174
Nolan, Christopher 171, 174
Nolland, John 17, 56, 59
Nouwen, Henri 19, 39, 48, 86, 88, 110,
115, 117, 130, 131, 142, 177, 184

Owen, John 15, 17
Owen, Wilfred 163, 172, 174

Pannenberg, W. 48
Pärt, Arvo 172
Pennington, M. Basil 130, 142
Perry, John 130, 143
Peter, St 24, 27, 31, 37, 38, 58, 143,
146, 177

Plato 18
Priestland, Gerald 174
Puhl, Louis J. 70

Rahner, Karl 18
Ramsey, Ian 59
Ramsey, Michael 26, 34, 69
Rees, Daniel 150, 157, 158
Richardson, Alan 59
Robertson, Edwin 174
Rodriguez, O. 99
Rogers, Carl 71
Rublev, Andrej 172
Russell, Anthony 104, 114, 115

Schwöbel, Christoph 19, 48
Seaborne, A. E. M. 130
Shaw, Gilbert 174
Simeon 10
Simon the Pharisee 39
Smith, Cyprian 34
Southwell, Robert 19
Spence, Alan 15
Spencer, Stanley 172
Stephen, St 86
Stephens, Simon 71
Stevenson, Kenneth 174

Stopfel, Barry 184

Taylor, Jeremy 171, 174
Tetley, Joy 131
Thérèse of Lisieux, St 158
Thielicke, Helmut 81
Thiselton, Anthony 83, 88
Thompson, Damian 173
Thompson, Francis 174
Thornton, Martin 8
Torrance, A. J. 48
Turner, Nigel 59

Vanier, Jean 59, 137, 142, 153, 157, 158,
    181, 184
Vanstone, W. H. ch. 7 *passim*, 100

Walsh, B. J. 48
Weil, Simone 167, 173, 181
West, Morris 48
Westcott, B. F. 107, 108, 115
White, Norman 174
Whyte, James 170
Wolters, Clifton 88
Wright, N. T. 18

Zechariah 25, 30
Zizioulas, J. 48

Subject Index

access ch. 3 *passim*, 170
accompaniment 109, 137, 148, 155, 156, 176
accountable/accountability 51, 105, 108, 113, 140, 154–6
Advisory Board of Ministry (Church of England) 118, 141, 158, 159, 174
Advisory Council for Church's Ministry (Church of England) 123, 125
anger 98, 109, 112
apprenticeship 127, 128
appropriate 14, 16, 36f, 43, 44, 51, 53, 54, 58, 60, 66, 80, 87, 93, 95, 107, ch. 11 *passim*, 135, 147, 156, 158, 178
art 161, 172
Ascension 74, 169
Aston Training Course 123
attentiveness 80, 138, 153
authentic 141, 151
authority 35, 37, ch. 5 *passim*, 64, 65, 74, 136, 139, 140, ch. 13 *passim*
conferred ch. 5 *passim*, 130, 138, 141, 150, 151
derived ch. 5 *passim*, 130, 138, 151
awareness 51, 82, 92
awesome 168

baptism 22, 52, 99, 157
of Jesus 15, 21–4, 37, 38, 58, 68, 89, 96, 106, 153, 155

being 62, 113, 114, 130
of God 144
Benedict's Rule 145
birth 9f, 18, 21, 22, 32, 37, 61, 68, 162
boundaries 107, 112, 113, 134, 149
bubblewrap, divine 11

choice 4, 5, 7, 14–16, 20, 33, 36, 44, 47, 50, 65, 66, 73, 75f, 81, 83, 87, 90, 112, 113, ch. 11 *passim*, 136, 162, 165, 181, 183, 184
chronos 81
Church
of England 118, 119, 127, 130, 141, 142, 165, 174
One 144, 157
Holy 144, 152
Catholic 144, 147, 157
Apostolic 144, 149, 157
circles of intimacy 29, 36, 40, 45, 66, 93
clown 47, 48, 151
collaborative ministry 141, 148, 156
commission 35, 52, 124, 170
community 4, 9, 12, 16, 17, ch. 4 *passim*, 64, 66, 78, 90, Part II *passim*
Community Development 81
companion 111, 113, 114, 137, 167, 184
condescending God 9–11, 17, 153
conflict 68, 89
consent 30, 54, 70, 91, 162, 183

188

consolation 69, 81, 94
constraint 95, 112
Continuing Ministerial Formation *see* formation
control 3, 5, 6 73, 79, 83, 105, 106, 166, 177, 178
covenant 31, 135, 138
critical distance 113, 116
cross 58, 65, 68, 80, ch. 8 *passim*, 94, 111, 160f, 163, 169, 172, 1/4
curacy 127, 128

darkness 7, ch. 3 *passim*, 76, 84, 87, 145, 179
deacon 41–4, 60, 69, 179
death 7, 55, 60, 68, 72, 74, 76, 82, 83, 88, 98, 108, 172, 173, 179, 183
delivering up *see* handed over
desert 23–5, 63, 64, 68, 96–8, 118, 182
desolation 81
discernment 6, 16, 35, 39, 43, 44, ch. 5 *passim*, 67, 78–81, 87, 93, 94, 124, 129, 130, chs. 12 and 13 *passim*, 165, 170, 181, 183
discipleship 6, 24
disclose/disclosure ch. 4 *passim*, 93, 99, 177
degrees of 36, 40, 93
Dominus Flevit ix, 183
drama 172
dunamis 51, 58

Easter 7, 29, 30
ecumenism 174
education 118, 119, 124, 125, 150
Edward King Institute for Ministry Development 159
emotion/emotional neutrality ch. 10 *passim*, 178, 183
empathy 26, 49, 106, 108, 113
emptiness 30–2, 63, 68, 69, 76, 87, 93 (*see also* kenosis)
enabler 73, 75, 79, 114, 139
enclosure 48, 135, 144, 157, 169

encounter 27, 28, 68, 69, 80, 134, 136, 144, 149, 157, 161, 162, 164f, 169
with God 61, 62
with others 63, 64, 132
ourselves 62
with world 152
enhypostasia 19
eschatology 85, 88
Eucharist 90, 149, 165, 171
evangelism 109, 115
exaltation 84
exousia 51
expectancy 78, 86, 161
experience 121, 139, 151, 154, 162, 170, 175, 176, 179, 181–3

face of Christ 47, 90, 168, 180
failure 42, 75, 122, 127, 146
fear 24, 47, 63, 64, 69, ch. 9 *passim*, 121, 130, 134, 152, 171, 179
finitude 63, 134
foot washing 39, 58, 133, 136, 143, 145, 147, 157, 169
forgiveness 64, 135, 143, 145–7, 177
formation 155
continuing ministerial 6, 114, ch. 11 *passim*
spiritual 153, 156
frailty 6, 7, 11, 14, 26, 51, 54, 56, 57, 63, 64, 67, 92, 98, 151
freedom 48, 59, 95, 112, 127, 136, 141, 153, 165, 166, 171, 180, 183
friendships 92, 139, 143, 176, 181
future 72, 77, ch. 8 *passim*

Gethsemane 22, 28, 68, 74, 80, 83, 97, 98, 169, 183
glory 22, 38, 54, 66, 74, 83, 88, 109, 143, 167–9
godfriends 67
Golgotha 94
grace 7, 16, 69, 78, 84, 85, 91, 96, 98, 99, 107, 118, 124, 133, 134, 137, 145, 146, 150

growth 21, 44, 45, 78, 112, ch. 11 *passim*, 134, 135, 147, 167

handed over 74, 80, 81, 91, 96–8, 132; *see also* paradidomi
healing 29, 55, 65, 86, ch. 9 *passim*, 109, 124, 135, 143, 145, 148, 158, 169, 178, 179
holiness 66, 95, 152, 154, 155, 170
holocaust 84
Holy Spirit 15f, 22, 23, 25, 27, ch. 4 *passim*, 51, 53, 73, 75, 83, 85, 91, 96, 106, 111, 113, 132, 135, 139–41, ch. 13 *passim*, 171
hope 6, 80, ch. 8 *passim*, 95, 109, 133, 179
hora 73f, 81
hour, the 73f, 80
humble/humility 6, ch. 6 *passim*, 162

identification 69, 108, 109, 111, 113, 184
identity 38, 46, 96, 115, 135, ch. 13 *passim*, 165, 174
idol 55, 97
illusions 63, 84, 94
Incarnation ch. 2 *passim*, 30, 36, 37, 149
integrity 53, 56, 120, 123, 131, 151
interdependence 38, 148
intimacy 17, 38, 46, 73, 95, 143, 144, 152, 153

joy 27, 29, 40, 62, 63, 76, 84, 114, 134, 144, 146, 153, 172, 180, 182

kairos 81
kenosis 13, 14, 21, 26, 31, 47, 57, 58, 61, 64, 79, 110, 149
knowledge chs. 10 and 11 *passim*, 169

leader/leadership 3, 6, 35, 38, 41, 48, ch. 5 *passim*, 66, 67, 76, 78, 80, 85, 87, 96, Part II *passim*
ordained 80, 118, ch. 13 *passim*, 169

learning 92, ch. 11 *passim*
listening 27, 32, 49, 54, 56, 67, 69, 78, 79, 87, 94, 95, 127, chs. 12 and 13 *passim*, 164, 170, 173, 178, 180
liturgy ch. 14 *passim*
Lockerbie Memorial Service 170
lonely 9
loneliness 63, 112, 137, 158
lonely place 150
longing 73, 78
love *passim*
agape 110
moderated 59, 110, 115

management theory 157
manipulation 4, 55, 63, 66, 79, 88, 107, 113, 126, 178
masks 4, 28, ch. 4 *passim*, 55, 90, 93, 130, 135, 137, 175, 182
meaning 87, 90, ch. 14 *passim*
intrinsic 162, 170
extrinsic 162, 170
mind of Christ 69, 70, 117, 165
ministry *passim*
mission 6, 110, 115, 135, 139, 141, ch. 13 *passim*
modernity 84
mystery 85, 144, 163, 168, 169, 173
music 27, 32, 161, 166, 172, 173

obedience 6, 15, 53, 58, 62–4, 69, 74, 75, 83, 104, 109, 138–40
ordination 103, 104, 146, 153

pain 5, 7, 14–16, 24, 26, 27, 31, chs. 4 and 6 *passim*, 81, ch. 8 *passim*, 89, 90, 92, chs. 10 and 14 *passim*, 178, 181, 182
paradidomi; 73f *see also* handed over
particular 39, 165
particularity 50, 56, 58, 110, 111, 126, 165
partnership ch. 13 *passim*
Passion, the 28, 29, 37, 38, 59, 73, 74, 115, 164

Subject Index

passive activity 58, ch. 7 *passim*, 113
pastoral care 42, 103, 104, 109, 113, 118,
    147, 149, 178
perfection 137
perichoresis 36, 66, 152, 164
Peterborough Project 131
Philippians 2:5–11 7, 12f, 22, 47, 60–3,
    83
porcupines 134, 135
post-modern 46–8, 88
power 3, 5, 7, 16, 37, 38, ch. 5 *passim*,
    65, 91, 98, 108, 110, 113, 176, 177, 179
    relinquishment of 50, 96, 98
    abuse of 49, 53, 113
powerlessness 9, 14, 51, 55, 56, 58, 70,
    75, 79, 114, 121, 132, 162, 184
prayer 6, 17, chs. 3 and 4 *passim*, 53,
    54, 56, 69, 70, ch. 7 *passim*, 82,
    87, 92–4, 113, Part II *passim*
preaching 3, 25, 28, 124, 150, 169, 170,
    177
presence 40, 163
present, being 60, 75, 113, 114, 135, 153
priest 42, 43, 57, 153, 156, 165, 171, 176,
    179, 183
priesthood 39, 59, ch. 13 *passim*, 176,
    177
primal love 68, 97
Prodigal Son, The 14, 81
professionalism 6, ch. 10 *passim*, 121,
    123, 124, 129, 155, 178
    characteristics of 104f, 108
promise 83, 85, 86, 88
prophetic activity 75, 79, 112, 120, 136
psychiatrist 92
psychologist 92, 137

redemption 45, 83, 167
reflection 30, 46, 52, 69, 70, 127–9, 138,
    139, 148, 150, 151, 168, 172, 177
relational 15, 17, 45, 51, 65, 125
relationship *passim*
residence 125f
resonance, divine ch. 14 *passim*, 181

resurrection 13, 29–32, 38, 65, 74, ch. 8
    passim, 146, 167, 169
reverence 62–4, 82
risk 22, 40, 41, 44, 52, 53, 56, 58, 63,
    68, 69, ch. 7 *passim*, 87, chs. 9
    and 10 *passim*, 125, 126, 129, 137,
    151, 157, 162, 171, 176, 180
Royal School of Church Music 59
rule 64, 70, 78, 81, 136, 145

sacrament 120, 161, 171
safe 87, 92, 134, 135, 161
salvation 11, 18, 144, 160, 167, 183
salvation history 83, 161, 165
secret place 21
self 5, 46, 47, 95, 96, 143
    true to 62, 150, 151, 164
self-emptying 7, ch. 2 *passim*, 47, 79,
    83, 84, 110, 117, 118, 120, 129, 177,
    179; *see also* kenosis
service ch. 6 *passim*, 72, 86, 88, 90, 111,
    113, 117, 118, 129, 136, 144, 147, 148,
    157, 161, 177, 180, 184
silence ch. 3 *passim*, 73, 76, 99, 114, 153,
    161, 169, 171, 173, 182
solidarity 108, 109
solitude 21, 22, 136, 150
spiritual direction 54, 66, 113, 130, 146,
    176, 178
status 52, 55, 66, 111
    of patient 59, 77, 81
stillness 23, 167
story 83, 135, 150, 163, 165, 175
struggle 64, 65, 83, 94, 97, 118, 121, 124,
    151, 170
submission 53, 57, 58, 62, 65, 82, 91
suffering 5, 7, 15, 16, 28, 31, 38, 54, 68,
    76, 83, 84, 86, 98, 108, 111, 113,
    139, 146, 156, 160f, 167, 172, 174
supervision 54, 67, 113, 156
support 67, 68, 87, 111, 113, 116, 121, 125,
    126, 129, 135–7, 155–8
    networks of 66

surrender 32, ch. 5 *passim*, 68, 73, ch. 9 *passim*, 115, 132, 181

symbol ch. 14 *passim*

Taizé 136, 159

tears ix, 3, 4, 8, 27, 48, 82, 109, 112, 168, ch. 15 *passim*
   of Jesus 8, 173, 183

technique 6, 106, 119, 122, 124, 129

temptation 63, 97
   of Jesus 8, 173, 183

theological reflection 119, 120, 128, 131

tradition 52, 74, 140, 145, 146, 156, 165

training 6, 69, 70, 92, 95, 97, 105, 106, 114, 115, 117, ch. 11 *passim*, 154, 156, 176, 177, 179
   context 121, 122, 125
   part-time 126, 127, 131, 138

Transfiguration 22, 26–8, 37, 68, 155, 169

transparency 4, 6, 32, 33, 50, 53, 124, 145, 169, 170, 176, 177, 181

Trinity, Holy ch. 2 *passim*, 36, 66, 90, 132, 134, 139, 144, 152–5, 164, 165, 172

trust 7, 22, 34, 41, 45, 46, 57, 58, 61, 68, 69, 79, 80, 83, 86, 87, 88, ch. 9 *passim*, 108, 121, 122, 125, 126, 137, 139, 155, 156, 176–8, 184

truth 7, 26, 27, 29, 40, 41, 44, 45, 49, 65, 93, 109, 120, 122, 138, 140, 141, 145, 161, 163, 165, 176

tutor 49, 121–3, 126

unconditional positive regard 67, 92, 155

universal 146, 150, 165, 166

victim 5, 45, 46, 55, 66, 73, 75, 83, 111, 156

vocation 6, 61, 64, 110, 117, 135, 137, ch. 13 *passim*, 164
   of Jesus 83, 153
   to be ourselves 61f, 64f, 153
   to love 103, 111, 112, 114
   to ministry 39, 93, 94

vulnerability *passim*
   as gift 83, 85–7, 94
   as idol 87
   definition of 4, 5, 90f

waiting 25, ch. 7 *passim*, 82, 87, 95, 113, 114, 140, 151, 180
   of Jesus 73
   passive 79
   temporal 73, 79

weakness 4, 5, 10, 11, 16, 40, 57, ch. 6 *passim*, 78, 85, 87, 97, 111–13, ch. 11 *passim*, 143, 148, 167, 170, 181

wilderness
   see desert

Word, the 29, 39, 110, 160, 170, 173
   'pickled in' 141, 142, 169

words 40, 46, ch. 14 *passim*

worship 3, 78, ch. 11 *passim*, 133, 138, 150, 152, ch. 14 *passim*, 176–8

wound 4, 5, 58, 65, 86, ch. 9 *passim*, 134, 148, 162, 164–6, 175, 179

'yes' 7, 29, 30, 33, 94, 95, 98